THE LION'S SHARE

A Combat Manual for the
• Divorcing Male •

THE LION'S SHARE

A Combat Manual for the
• *Divorcing Male* •

J. ALAN ORNSTEIN

Times
BOOKS

Grateful acknowledgment is made to the authors and publishers for permission to reprint the following material:

"First Fig," by Edna St. Vincent Millay, from *Collected Poems*, published by Harper & Row, copyright © 1922, renewal © 1950 by Edna St. Vincent Millay. Excerpt from "Please Make Up Your Mind," p. 104 by Allen-Merrell-Ornstein. Reprinted by permission of the publisher, Wanessa Music, Inc. (BMI). Excerpts from "Alumnus Football," by Grantland Rice, from *The Final Answer and Other Poems*. Reprinted by permission of the publisher, A.S. Barnes & Company, Inc. Excerpt from "Caution," by Norman Savage, first published in *Scree* magazine. Reprinted by permission of the poet. Excerpt from *Some Men Are More Perfect than Others* by Merle Shain, copyright © 1973 by Merle Shain. Reprinted by permission of Paul R. Reynolds, Inc., 12 East 41 Street, New York, N.Y. 10017. Excerpt from *I, the Jury* by Mickey Spillane, copyright © 1947 by E.P. Dutton & Co., Inc. renewal © 1975 by Mickey Spillane. Reprinted by permission of the publisher.

Library of Congress Cataloging in Publication Data

Ornstein, J. Alan.
  The lion's share: a combat manual for the divorcing male.

  1. Divorce—United States.   2. Divorcees.
3. Single men.   I. Title.
HQ834.074   1978   301.42'84   77-87833
ISBN 0-8129-0754-X

FOR FANTA
in memoriam

Contents

. CONTENTS .

Acknowledgments

My sincere gratitude is extended to all those friends and colleagues who encouraged me with their enthusiasm during this project.

I deeply appreciate the information given me by Darryl Klay, private investigator; the comments of Dr. Irving Handelsman; the myth of the writer created long ago by Dan Curley and Lowell Johnson, then of Syracuse University; the diligent and pain-staking efforts of Anne Foley as research assistant; the devotion, humor and commentary of Ellen Green, who was the first to copy the manuscript; the continuing education provided by my sons and daughters, Nicole, Kirk, Kathy, Scott and Bruce, without whom writing many parts of the book and particularly the chapter "Heirs and Heiresses Apparent" would have been totally impossible; the early unshakable faith of Joan and Joe Foley, my agents and dedicated supporters; and all those anonymous men whose lives I've shared as attorney and friend through their marital suffering.

Finally, a negative—to all of the "Bitches of Buchenwald" without whose female chauvinistic greed the need to express a clear male point of view would never have arisen.

You are not permitted to kill a woman who has wronged you, but nothing forbids you to reflect that she is growing older every minute. You are avenged 1,440 times a day.

AMBROSE BIERCE

rebach (rē-bach) *n*: A rebachelor. A man becoming a bachelor again, generally after a divorce.

Monthly vital statistic report published by the United States National Center of Health Statistics for the 12-month period August 1976 through July 1977:

MARRIAGES:	2,160,000
DIVORCES:	1,079,000

THE LION'S SHARE

*A Combat Manual for the
• Divorcing Male •*

Prologue

This is not a fair or gentle book. It is not intended to be well-mannered. It lacks in-depth sociological research and may not deserve scholarly evaluation; but it is accurate and it is honest. It is written for the benefit of the male chauvinist and will be of very little value to other folk. It presents an entirely masculine point of view and is defensible solely on that basis.

The term "rebach" defines the divorcing American male, regardless of where the trip to the divorce court has been made (or by whom), and no matter what the grounds (he cheated on, beat up, or abandoned his wife—or she did these things to him). Young or old, rich or poor (but certainly he will be poorer than when he started), if there is a divorce, he is a "rebach." This subject, then, is the man who has made the complete circle from single freedom to marriage and is back again at the starting point, a bachelor. The difference is that by now he is like a retreaded tire—slightly used, somewhat battered, but with plenty of wear still left, even though he may not discover that to be a fact right away.

·1·

In the Beginning
He Took a Rib

In the beginning there were the words that got you married. In the end there are the words that conclude the problem (that marriage has become):

> "I love you, but I'm no longer in love with you."
> "I'll fight to save the marriage."
> ". . . for the sake of the children . . ."
> "You must see a marriage counselor." ("You go. I don't need one.")
> "How will I tell my parents? They love you like their own son." ("What the hell do they have to do with the whole thing?")
> "How can you do this? I've given you everything."
> "What does that mean? We fuck!" ("That's fucking?")
> "Look what we have gone through together."
> And rarely, but with luck, "I hate your stinking guts. Get out!"

And so the words are said. They are all clichés and they have been said a thousand times before, but when you are hearing them or saying them, you think they are original, or at the very least appropriate to the occasion. It takes these words or words similar to these to move the idea of divorce from an abstract wishful prayer into a not unthinkable reality.

If you spoke them, then you have simultaneously with the words grown a set of horns. If you have been the recipient, you walk with a halo. With a halo you can feel righteousness, rage, and resentment. (Great healthy feelings.) If you are wearing horns, guilt. (Not so good.)

In any case, all of the emotions, though seemingly real at moments, are actually beside the point. In the moments of sanity that only occasionally prevail in this early stage will come recognition of the aggravation that you lived with: a sexless sex life without erections, and a contemplated future of gritted teeth, exhaustion, and high blood pressure.

Thus with certain words, your marriage has ended. The abortive efforts called "trial separation," "separate vacations," or any other method generating time apart are really the first steps to just being apart. Apart is a step taken with proper solemnity, but inside the screams of relief exceed anything ever heard or felt in a bedroom in ultimate sexual abandonment. The greatest advantage of this first moment of freedom, be it two weeks or six months, is that it allows you to see clearly just how rotten living with this woman has been.

For one thing, you don't have to go home to her, which means that you don't have to look at her or be near her. Suddenly you have time to look at, talk to, and be near other women who, surprisingly enough, will be interested in looking at, talking to, and being near you. This great freedom will only be disrupted by your unaccountable desire from time to time to call your wife, which you will do. Such conversations will be totally aggravating, inconsequential, and overly long. Your wife's calls to you will accomplish exactly the same thing—nothing!

The return from this "trial separation" or "separate vacation" will result in serious contemplation of the marriage with a great deal of emphasis placed on the word communication. You should realize that communication was best understood by Alexander Graham Bell and that discussion of the topic should be handled by means of his invention, the telephone. If you have to discuss communication, you will never have it. It is also important to understand that the family doctor and/or minister cannot help you now and that marriage counselors and psychiatrists can only be helpful in the future. As to the past, it is too late even to learn basic Morse Code.

·2·

Lawyers: Knights in Rusted Armor

Don't give in to guilt! As you slam the front door to leave, it is well to remind yourself of all the reasons why *you* are walking out, and not she. Certainly if there are children around, you don't want to lock her out and be stuck with the kids. Except in that case, however, there is no real reason why you shouldn't change the locks before she does, unless she is not working and would have no place to go except to her mother's, your mother-in-law, and really you can't be *that* angry. At this stage, it is suggested that you consult a lawyer. In connection with that choice consider the following:

Do not retain a friend, particularly a mutual friend of you and your wife.

Do not look to the attorneys who handle your business affairs.

Do not retain a woman attorney, whose attitude may be more liberated than legalistic.

Find a lawyer who specializes in divorce and meet him. If he is tough and views this as a business problem only, retain him.

Avoid attorneys who ask you:

"Are you sure you want this?"

.LAWYERS: KNIGHTS IN RUSTED ARMOR.

"Do you realize the seriousness of this step?"
"Have you considered the children?"
"Why not try again?"

Seek a lawyer who will spend enormous quantities of time listening to the equally enormous quantities of useless information you will feed him and who, at least in the beginning, will be readily available by phone.

Do not be misled by your wife's simple statement that she doesn't want to hurt you, she only wants enough to live on. In situations like this one, such a statement is self-contradicting, and will create an insoluble dilemma.

Honesty with your lawyer is imperative. However, your inclination will be to lie and to describe what a super human being you have been and how wronged you were. Understand that the more of that nonsense you tell a lawyer, the more time the problem will take, the higher the cost will run.

Don't be noble.

If you have struck your wife, pray no witnesses come forth and that there are no visible scars. If you have a girlfriend, acknowledge it and don't be concerned if your lawyer appears to feel some sympathy for your wife. Even if you feel that the breakup is fully your fault and that she has been Joan of Arc, you must be assured that his attitude will be professional and that he will approach the problem as if your wife were the abominable snowman (snowperson?).

Be assured also that when he is in contact with your wife's attorney he will describe you in brilliant hues. In any event, it's all hogwash. The name of the game at this point is strictly dollars. If he can manage it, he will arrange to give her nothing. If he should be successful, don't worry about it, for you can always give her more (and you should be so lucky). It is not helpful to shrug your shoulders and tell your lawyer, "What the hell, she can't get blood from a stone." The fact is she can. Incidentally, in spite of what anybody tells you, including your lawyer, do not consider becoming a monk. It is not realistic. Monking without adequate practice is difficult, and there are many other ways of avoiding an adultery rap.

As much as you may feel that your matrimonial problem is special and unlike any other that has ever occurred in or out of this world, your lawyer will assure you that the only thing that is unique about your problem is your name, face, and bank balance. Beyond that, there is very little that you have gone through, are going through, or will go through that every soon-to-be divorced man has not experienced. You won't accept this and will continue to believe that you are the exception to the rule.

You will hardly be the first man to say grimly, almost tearfully, voice cracking, "I want custody." But in fact you don't really want custody, you just think it's appropriate to say. What in God's name are you going to do with children as a bachelor? Of course, you may feel that you are the exception. At this stage you are convinced your wife is psychotic, or at least crazy, and a damn lousy mother. Certainly Dick and Jane would be better off with you than with her. Even Spot would be better off with you. (These are not unique feelings either.)

She is not, and they won't be. Let us reason the situation out. Even if your wife spends considerable time dating (thus leaving the children alone), and even if she makes love in the bedroom next to the children's bedroom, and even if you don't like the way she dresses or feeds them, she will still be better for them than you. For, should you, the father, be unlucky enough to achieve custody, which rarely happens, you would then be substituting for a mother, not a father. As a maid, you would be expected to feed and clothe them; as a weekend father you would find them interfering with a bachelor life that you have barely begun to enjoy. Remember that so long as you only have visitation rights, and not custody, you can emerge the good guy. All you have to do is show up with circus and movie tickets and gifts and hope like hell that your wife doesn't get smart and decide to be the good guy, sticking you with custody. Being a good guy is a cinch; being a parent isn't. Adequate opportunity to visit with your children is more than sufficient compensation and even then, don't struggle to make that time too generous, for you will feel an obligation more to them than to yourself.

This is destructive.

It is not destructive, however, to allow your lawyer to say to his worthy adversary, "My client feels that your client is an unfit mother; hence, we are seeking custody." The psychological pressure you are placing on the woman, even though the outcome is inevitable, should be reflected in the ultimate economic settlement.

Other clever ploys include a threat to leave the state or, if you are desperate, the country. You will be believed by your wife, if not by her lawyer. Nevertheless, her lawyer will feel the pressure that your wife will exert, and any time her lawyer feels pressure you have scored points.

Even before slamming the front door or consulting that lawyer, collect all financial papers, including cancelled checks and American Express bills. (Gather up old love-letters, too, if you were stupid enough to leave such items around.)

Transfer all savings from those accounts that were joint with you and your wife when you were planning to buy the vacation cottage into your own account at a bank that she has never heard of. And don't worry if some, most, or all of that money is hers: you can always give it back.

If you have a safe-deposit box, find your way to it and function like a vacuum cleaner. Take everything, including your marriage license. If the vault contains jewelry that you have given her, take that. (However, if there is jewelry inherited from her mother or her second cousin twice removed, leave it alone. She will be only angry with respect to most everything else, but she can become a female Jack the Ripper over her great-grandmother's diamond tiara.)

Do not for one moment assume that she does not want to get rid of you and that only you want to dump her.

.LAWYERS: KNIGHTS IN RUSTED ARMOR.

Assume that the feeling is equal. It doesn't make any difference. All you are doing is taking some early steps to assist in a "business" negotiation.

Repetitious or not, it's worth restatement. Just as you can always take more, you can always give it back.

The key to a successful financial arrangement is your "knight in rusted armor." If your lawyer thinks of himself as a defender of the cause or as a "knight in shining armor," you could be in big trouble. Take the case of those Knights of the Round Table who chased the Holy Grail. Their armor was polished—their actions futile. It is one thing for *you* to rant and rave and carry on emotionally. But if you have a lawyer who adopts a "vendetta" attitude ("I'll get him" or "I'll stick this case up his ass") when referring to your wife's lawyer, it is probably time to go elsewhere.

You want a lawyer who is highly motivated because that motivation can bring about a great agreement. But you do not want a lawyer who will, as a result of his own ego or pique or because your wife's lawyer said "fuck you" to him, turn an ordinary matrimonial civil war into an explosive do-or-die end-of-the-world holocaust. In spite of the fact that you may enjoy the ranting and raving of a lawyer going slightly lunatic (and you may even think that this is the way it ought to be), if your lawyer is habitually overwrought, his fits will probably extend the time your agreement will take by many months. You must have a lawyer who, after pressing all the psychological buttons (with your help), will know when to settle. The obvious time for settlement is when

.13.

your first psychological master stroke (whatever that might be) has been effective and your wife knows it. Even though your inclination will be to press even further now that you're ahead, your lawyer will tell you that the only time you *can* settle is when you *are* ahead.

Litigation—at best unpredictable, at worst destructive—should be avoided. Your lawyer should appear ready, however, to go into court without hesitation at the drop of a nasty word.

Even the best lawyers need to be motivated. It is useful to tell a lawyer that he is terrific and that you trust his judgment calls. But it is absolutely imperative that you analyze these decisions.

Be aware of the fact that lawyers weary of cases. When you see that happening, recognize that the case has probably gone on too long and that it may be time to sit with him and renegotiate his fee. (In other words, paying more can pay off.)

A lawyer will know when the end of a case is in sight, even though his client won't and will still be crying for blood. Be sure you are aware of what is going on and that you stay aware. When the pieces of a settlement fall into place, there will be an almost audible click.

A cardinal rule: under no circumstances pay your wife's lawyer in advance. Unfortunately, more often than not you will wind up paying your wife's lawyer in the end. Because you (if you were smart) have already tied up all of the family's funds, your wife's ability to pay him in advance is, at best, limited. His staying power may be considerably less than that of the lawyer who is well paid. If your wife has felt financial pressures and is hungry, and if your wife's attorney has been poorly paid and is hungry, a settlement may come about more quickly.

Your wife has probably made only a small partial payment to her lawyer. You must consider the balance of her lawyer's fee as ransom money, and ransom money is never paid without assurance that the body will be returned alive and kicking. Any lawyer who receives only a small payment in advance will begin to treat a case as old business and look for new business. The money he has received has been spent and respent and he still needs to pay office overhead. The perfect arrangement would be to negotiate the legal fee with your ex-wife's attorney three months after the matter is complete—after he has already poured his blood and sweat and her tears into it.

If she has money of her own, you have a problem.

Though women tend to have almost blind trust in their lawyers, the average woman can prove to be a difficult client. Women have a tendency to run in wolf packs and to take advice one from the other. (Men tend not to do this.) Your wife will "edit" the advice she hears from other divorced or soon-to-be-divorced women, using only that which seems suitable. Her half-baked ideas can screw up settlements that may have taken months to achieve. At this point you can hope that your wife is being represented by a competent male chauvinist lawyer. He can educate your wife to the fact that marriage and subsequent divorce are not a lifetime pension plan for her.

Parenthetically, whatever you've heard about divorce kits you can forget, unless you were married with a kit. A kit can never anticipate the innumerable pitfalls which await the unschooled. Most important, a kit cannot negotiate with your wife.

Many cases reach a point where the lawyers realize it is time to end; nothing more will be accomplished. Keeping in mind that they will meet on other cases in the future, they reach a settlement and then press their clients (literally, they team up) to close.

It is incredible how often a husband and wife who have come to a bitter parting will nevertheless agree between themselves not to tell their lawyers certain things. These can cover the gambit from sexual aberrations to shared but hidden assets. It is important that you arrange such an agreement if you can do so. But it is equally important that your promise to her to maintain absolute secrecy be a total lie.

Deceit can be a useful tool in a "business" negotiation.

In preparation of a total rear guard action, it is well to begin convincing your wife that you are broke. When you have made the total decision to split, and before you have told her, begin having trouble paying bills (department stores, landlords, mortgages). Discontinue as many credit cards as possible to which she has access. If you have a full-time maid, suggest that you can only afford one part-time. If you have a part-time maid, tell your wife that you can only afford babysitters. If you have babysitters, proclaim that you can't afford them, and suggest, solely for effect, that that's what she should be doing anyhow. In addition, having created the proper atmosphere, convince your wife that she should get a job to help pay the bills, if she is not already working. If she is working, convince her to work harder. (From a practical point of view, the dollars that she will start to earn will be deemed part of her total income when support and alimony requirements are considered.)

As to the negotiations, leave them to your solicitor. No matter how good you think you have been in your business life as a negotiator, accept the simple fact that if you mess around with this one you will have a fool for a client. Do not discuss any of the negotiations with your wife unless directed to do so by your attorney. If possible, since she probably never directly negotiated anything before in her life, limit your involvement to the division of furniture and other joint personal property such as wedding presents. Talk in terms of dividing everything, even those things *she* brought to the marriage. Maintain this posture throughout the heat and strife of the total negotiation, thereby distracting her from the consequential things such as support, alimony, insurance, etc. Ultimately, if you handle yourself well, you should come out of the marriage with the following items: all of your clothes; the pictures of the children; the stereo and hi-fi equipment plus records; some of the art on the walls; the books in the house, except cookbooks (but in self-defense you ought to take one); various and sundry sporting equipment, i.e., baseball bats, tennis rackets, ice skates, skis; and your camera equipment.

If you get anything beyond that, you are an unusual, strange breed who has achieved far more than the average. If you have plans to acquire any of the furniture, it would be well that you opt for the den furniture (if there is a den) and the beds from the extra bedroom (if there is an extra bedroom). These items will help furnish a new apartment. A sometimes successful ploy is to become highly emotional about your own special favorite chair (even if you've never really considered it a favorite).

A word of advice with respect to what to anticipate when the document, the oft-referred-to "separation agreement," is finally complete and ready for signatures. At that meeting, but prior to your picking up a pen, you must maintain a posture that you are just signing another contract similar to those you've signed all your life. It is just another business deal.

It is just another business deal.

God damn it, it is just another business deal!

Thus when you meet your wife in her lawyer's office, you will be truly composed. (You will always meet in her lawyer's office because the idiotic mores of the legal profession require that most negotiations be conducted at the office of the lawyer of the wife.)

If the lawyers involved are clever, you will sit in one room and your wife will sit in another while final changes in the papers are made. But however clever the

lawyers are, after having resolved a multitude of details, there will surely be left some minor unresolved crap— who gets the Kewpie doll won at Coney Island or who gets the parakeet. The resolution of these major points will require that both you and your wife meet around a desk with the attorneys.

Your wife will be immaculately groomed, looking as well as she possibly can—better than you've ever seen her, in a new suit with professional makeup and a becoming hairdo. The conversation, after a simple greeting, will be almost nonexistent, except that when her lawyer says, "We have resolved everything except the Kewpie doll and the parakeet," your wife will reach out, gently touch your hand, and say, "I've given you everything." Still maintaining your business composure, you will say quietly, "Bullshit, you have gotten everything."

She will look shocked and jerk back in her chair. Meanwhile, the lawyers will exchange looks of despair as they watch months of time and work coming apart and contemplate indefinite delays in the payment of their fees.

However, fear not; the documents will be signed. (You get the Kewpie doll and she keeps the parakeet.)

As quickly as possible, you will get the hell out. You will probably have delivered to your wife's attorney the fee that has been held out as a carrot. You will consider the fee outrageous, but if the man was competent you've at least got room to live. If he wasn't competent, you probably wound up in court. The courts will almost always give a wife less than she can get in a settlement (unless the settlement is improper). But the emotional shock dealt to the psyche by the public venting of beefs and the displaying of dirty linen negates any slight advantage that a court settlement might have for you. It is also sad to report that the courts are becoming more liberally disposed toward giving a wife a reasonable break.

After you have stormed out of the office, you will do one of a number of things.

You will adjourn with your lawyer to his club and have a drink or two or three.

You will feel an enormous letdown, the same kind of letdown felt in other situations when you have waited to accomplish something and finally it has occurred.

You may, hoping to forget the recent grim encounter, seek out a woman and find solace in bed.

Slowly you will begin to forget. You will mourn the past for what it might have been and look forward with anticipation to the future. You have finally cut bait and are now entering the first stage of rebaching.

·3·

The Only True Aphrodisiac

The papers are signed, or the court has delivered its decree, and you are now a free man, though the view ahead is not terribly clear. Looking back, however, you cannot forget those early stages when you assumed the role of adulterer because the pain of marriage was so great, and the only great escape was other women. You had no choice but to become an adulterer.

In the early stages of adultery you have to be particularly careful in your choice of women. However, there is really no safe female. With any outside relationship you run the risk of further complicating your already complicated marriage.

There are, of course, four brands of female available to you. They are nationally known and recognized as single, married, divorced, and professional. With the last it's uncomplicated—solely a matter of money. Such a relationship carries with it limited chance of exposure (other than to medically treatable diseases) and can be handled with a clever *nom de plume*. She won't care if you're Joe Smith, John Doe, or Martin Chuzzlewit. If she is any good, she should be able to satisy you both physically and emotionally, because a professional who has learned her art will understand the need for the proper lie. This lie will encompass your indefatigable appetite, your suave personality, your great sensitivity, and, of course, your generosity (which generosity will be directly proportionate to the extent and scope of her lies).

Dealing with the others presents in each case various nuances.

The married woman is probably the safest of all. She may very well be your wife's best friend, but will rarely be the wife of your best friend. This is a strange phenomenon, explained only by the fact that female friendships tend to lack the loyalty characteristic of friendships between males. (Males early on develop a sense of locker room loyalty that females do not understand or enjoy.) She is out for a fling, friendship be damned. She will justify her infidelity in one of two ways: either her marriage is lousy or it was one of those things she never meant to happen. The latter is a bald-faced lie, but she will continue to enjoy the relationship, as will you. You will only be "found out" if this woman has a falling out with your wife and in a fit of anger tells all. This will bring to her face a cat-that-swallowed-the-canary look, and the same cat will be out of the bag.

The standards of single and divorced females are fairly similar, except that the single person may be exceedingly naive and highly romantic, while the divorcée will move with extraordinary guilt, her sole purpose being to be around to pick up the pieces (that is, you) when your marriage finally shatters (from her point of

view, the sooner the better). In both cases, stay away from women in the office. Constant proximity to your lover is frustrating because it limits your extramarital activities just to her. It also can be more than you bargained for.

In a relationship with the single woman (a highly volatile romantic relationship), her speeches will include the following phrases:

"I want nothing from you except to live for the moment."

"If our relationship becomes too involved, we will end it but always remain friends."

"I expect nothing from you. It would be stupid if it were otherwise."

The sense of the romantic will control her mind. At some point, the fact that you must often leave her and return to your wife's bed, sometimes hurriedly after making love, will begin to bug her. Because your meetings will occur, for obvious reasons, at lunch or cocktail time, and never on weekends and rarely in the evenings, she will be lonely in the evenings, buggy on weekends, and miserable on holidays. After a while she may begin to want you to make a choice between her and the soon-to-be ex-wife (in other words, she is becoming as possessive as hell). This is a choice you are hardly ready, willing, or able to consider, never mind to make.

The divorcée has been through it all. Her attitude is hard-nosed, her approach calculating. She will, if she uses her head, play you like a fish on a string, knowing full well that your marriage is now over (probably before even you know it), and be content to bide her time.

She will be tough, clearly the tougher of the two, though she will be subtle. In both cases, but for different reasons, if either of these women is offended, she will find a way to let your wife know about her presence in your life.

There are two clear "do nots." Do not write. Do not take pictures. If you write, do not mail the letter. Read it to her. If you take pictures, keep the negatives. The only picture anybody should get is a picture of herself which does not include you.

The fear of being caught is generally great but, in truth, not realistic. However, it helps if you fantasize.

Fantasize the entrapment, fantasize your capture, fantasize your being seen together, fantasize all possible circumstances that might require explanation. Then prepare your defense in advance. (The wilder the story, the more believable it will be, for she will only want to believe your innocence.)

But think the big lie—denial at all cost, no matter how ludicrous the denial may be. Deny. Deny. Deny.

And think Detective.

The possibility of your being followed by a detective is very slight because such surveillance is extremely costly. However, if you think that somebody may be detecting, there are things that you can do to protect yourself.

An awareness (at all times) of the possibility is critical. It is virtually impossible, short of the expenditure of gigantic funds or blind luck, for you to be successfully followed if you do not establish patterns. The more patterns to your life, the easier it is to follow you and to know when not to bother following you. If you generally go to the gym at 8:00, start going at 9:30.

Don't ever be seen with a woman if you think Big Brother is watching you.

Being followed in any large town usually requires two people, generally a man and a woman. They will probably follow you by sitting in a car.

There are simple things you can do to determine whether, in fact, somebody is waiting to tail you.

If you leave your apartment on foot, see if anyone in the immediate area gets out of a car and starts walking behind you. If so, buy a newspaper and return to your apartment.

If you really want to do it French Connection style, start on foot, then get on a subway or a bus. One of the two people following you must then get out of a car and get on the bus or subway. Just as he or she boards, you suddenly get off. Just like on television, it works!

If you know that you are being followed and you know who is following you, walk over and say hello. This requires the detectives to bring in a new team of followers, thus allowing you a cooling-off period. Never expect a detective who is caught to admit that, in fact, he is following you.

You can also hire your own detective to follow you over a prescribed route, and he will be able to determine very quickly if you are being followed. This, however, costs money.

If you are in a car, *do not* go through a Kojak-style wild driving scene to lose the detectives. First, they may decide on their own to disappear. Second, you can kill yourself.

One of the truly great ways to get rid of a tail is to allow a detective to assume that you have completed your activities and are home for the evening. Then three or four hours later go out. The normal detective will have gone home to bed by that time, having reported to his employer that you were in.

When you drive a car regularly, do not park near to where you pick up your woman friend. A detective often begins following you by watching your car.

Understanding the limitations of a private detective is the key to successful adultery. Regardless of how effective a private detective is and how much experience he has, he doesn't know you, aside from a possible look at a four-year-old passport photo. You can throw the average private detective with a simple change in your external appearance—wear a new hat or substitute a greatcoat for a pea jacket. The detective gets to a point where he isn't following you, he is following a coat. It doesn't take much to change your appearance, and if you are clever, he may not be able to see you at all from 100 yards.

Another thing to remember is that there are detectives who do not use their legs or their eyes and who must instead use simple ploys. There are ways of determining whether a door has been opened. A piece of paper or a match jammed in the door and later found lying on the floor will indicate that somebody has been checking your door.

Last minute changes in means of travel (car to plane, car to train) are effective but often hard to arrange.

After twelve or fourteen hours, the detective, like anybody else, is tired. If you have had an opportunity to sleep during that period, you may be able to break him down.

A man traveling around on a weekend is almost impossible to stay with because of the complexity of our transportation system. A man who does not depend on a car is much more difficult to track than one who constantly uses an automobile.

A huge apartment complex with its banks of elevators is absolutely defeating to a detective because it is virtually impossible for him to determine where you may have disembarked.

Finally, phone taps and electronic bugging are really not in vogue at the present time. It is too easy for a detective to blow a license, and wiretapping is a felony. A detective who would suggest such means to a client has to be a rank amateur.

One or two other hot tips. When you are calling a girlfriend long distance, don't use your office or home phone. These records can be subpoenaed. Use a pay phone and pay cash. Don't use your credit card. If you speak often over the telephone, have her call you.

Don't register in a motel or hotel as Mr. and Mrs.,

and whenever possible, bypass public and quasi-public accommodations. For lovemaking, use an apartment a friend sets up, or better still, use a friend's apartment.

One final tip. Great sources of information for all detectives are doormen. A doorman approached by a detective with a ten-dollar bill can be extremely helpful to him, especially if you have been an S.O.B. to the doorman. So treat doormen courteously, be friendly, and tip well.

The doorman is not above taking the detective's $10.00 and expecting $20.00 from you. If he has reason to believe that he might get $20.00 from you for the same information, he will be delighted to come to your door immediately after the detective leaves and share with you all the answers the private detective just paid $10.00 for. The approach to a doorman is a double-edged sword.

•4•

You Are a Common Denominator

Rebach is a three-stage affair. It begins with the physical separation. This is a period of wallowing in guilt, self-doubt, boredom, anxiety, and loneliness. You spend much of your time figuring out how to get your laundry done.

The second stage is one of women and sex and *Playboy* magazine.

The third stage is one of settled attitudes and relationships. Rebach no more!

In other words, the first stage is the woman, the second stage is women, and the third stage is the woman.

If you have seen one rebach, you have seen them all. If you have heard one rebach, you have heard them all. But telling this to a rebach and making him understand it is impossible.

"How can you say that I'm the same as everybody else? I'm not."

"I'm much more sensitive than most people."

"I'm much brighter . . ."

"I have greater interests and elaborate hobbies."

"My wife was crazier."

. THE LION'S SHARE .

"I make more money . . ."

Every rebach acts exactly like every other rebach; the only thing that changes is their size and shape. They do everything in a similar fashion and react identically under certain circumstances. They are great sufferers, are habitually defensive, are hostile, sentimental, egocentric, guilt-ridden, oversexed, and impotent. All in proper turn. During their rebach period they live a life of the lost.

They suffer from lack of money (or from the constant threat of lack of money) because they gave too much away to their ex-wife (or they think they did).

They defend their reasons for getting a divorce to envious married men who think they would like to be rebached themselves and who, in one way or another, show their resentment of the rebach's new freedom.

They are alternately hostile toward the Bitch of Buchenwald (prior wife), sentimental about their previous marriage, and concerned because they cannot decide whether to be hostile or sentimental.

They are guilty about everything.

They are oversexed, even though they may not act out their sexual desires, and as frequently as not they are impotent.

They are you, a rebach. As you enter the first stage of rebach, you are a mass of gigantic contradictions and confusions. No matter what you do, there is no escape, for nothing has prepared you for this part of your life.

It is a period when you will hang by your thumbs. All the explanations of what you are going through (and seeing all the others going through) will do very little to help. There are no continuing education courses given today which teach you how to hang by your thumbs. It is painful. It is real. It is happening. And it will be identical for those that follow.

This initial phase is also a period of total lack of confidence which you will try to conceal by behaving enormously egocentric and arrogant. Those who recognize this behavior will tell you that you are compensating. Your automatic nasty response will be that you don't need any "five-cent psychiatry."

Finally, the initial phase carries with it boredom. The glory days envisioned of wine, women, sex, sex, wine, women are nonexistent. But fear not—they are coming!

The next stage is that of woman. Not any woman, but *the* woman. Happily not the ultimate woman, just a woman who is, on the surface at least, super understanding, super smart, and a super lay. She will likely be followed by other women. Each of these in their turn will become *the* woman and each will be super everything. This is a stage that is characterized by absolute fidelity—to the current woman while she lasts.

In about a year from go, rarely less, you will escape into another also highly irrational period, the second stage. A fantasy life, but creative. You will seek to create and build around yourself the great playboy image and to reflect this image in the way you walk, talk, dress, live, think. You will become a fond and arrogant believer in the basic principle of selfishness and you will justify it. You will become a walking copy of *Playboy* magazine at its best and worst. You will be subject only to the whims of your own imagination, and you will slowly dispose of many of the first stage miseries. You will have quickly disposed of that first woman to seek women at large. You will easily become a male chauvinist sexist pig and you will wonder what's so bad about that. With luck, you will maintain that mantle for the rest of your life, for it is a title which indicates you have developed independence of thought, spirit, and energy, not subject to female whimsy or calculation. You have won over the impulse to be known as thoughtful and liberated. You have made the ultimate male statement.

Sanity will return with experience and learning, and with it you will reach the third and final stage of rebach, the one that will permit honest relationships and eliminate much of the second stage characteristics evidenced by conversations that required total unlimited self-centered ego and began:

"I do . . ."
"I know . . ."
"I can . . ."
"I want . . ."
"I will . . ."
"I think . . ."
"I should . . ."
"I should not . . ."
"I remember . . ."

Much time will have passed. You will have spent a great deal of money. You will have achieved very little, but all of that is behind you. You will have your head on straight, more or less. Your life will be easier, more comfortable, and quite livable.

Just as there is a prologue for every rebach, that is to say, words, separation, and divorce, so also is there an epilogue. But the epilogue does not carry with it the universality of the prologue.

If the rebach has progressed, moved, blundered, or staggered through the various stages of rebachelorhood, including the bewildering first stage, the properly manic second, and the calm of the third, then it is possible to enter into a period just something less than perfect. It is a period in which a single female relationship will have developed. If you have not become a hermit, and if you have not gotten mired in gross hostility toward women (which in general they may well deserve from you), and if you have matured and grown wiser due to experience, this relationship will develop. Whether you believe it or not, you will grow.

It is inescapable.

That does not, however, mean that the relationship must turn into marriage. Nor does it mean that you are having an affair. It merely means that you have found a woman who, for the moment, is comfortable. That moment is one chapter in everyone's life. It need not be extended into the book of marriage.

·5·

One Initial on the
Shower Curtain and Towels

The opening line in the first act is:

"Free at last. Free at last. Thank God Almighty, free at last."

Free of what? Well, at the very least free of the Bitch of Buchenwald. Free also to relieve seminal pressures that may have reached a point of intolerance. This freedom, of course, does not assume that through all of what has gone before you remained a vestal virgin. But if occasionally you checked into a hotel as husband and "wife," the act always carried with it the imagined threat of the hotel detective.

This paranoia, ridiculous but prevalent in an adulterous liaison, breeds suspicious looks at doormen in buildings of friends' borrowed apartments. It also breeds fear in her apartment that a friend will appear and she will have to introduce you. God forbid that the friend should realize that you and she are committing adultery.

You are free now also to do what every woman assumes is a man's right, privilege and special advantage: you can go to a bar alone and stare at yourself in the mirror behind the bar, intent on looking either seriously perturbed or deeply contemplative ($E=mc^2$). With the disproportionate male to female ratio in the bar, you hope to God as the door opens that it's a woman and that there is a seat next to you and that six other men whose lines are better, and who are better looking, better dressed, and have more money, will not descend on her and gain her attention first. This special privilege is used by women as an explanation for why divorce is easier for a man than for a woman. "He can always go to a bar by himself."

You are now free to find a new and attractive apartment, though you must also deal with the other complexities of life such as acquiring furniture, doing the laundry, hiring a maid if you can afford one, and meeting females.

Your first apartment will be the apartment you grabbed in a hurry when you left. If you have been smart, you have either furnished it with Salvation Army specials or you have spent a minimum of dollars at a chain department store that supplied everything in one fell swoop.

Better yet, you have leased entire suites of furniture with the option to buy (you never will). They are clean and modern or pseudo-something, and they help this first apartment to achieve a modern plastic fast-food look. Delivery is immediate, cash outlay minimal, and the total effect is one of "a room full of furniture."

The wall-to-wall carpeting will be so scratchy that walking on it in bare feet will require you to invade the Band-Aid box. The bed, critical, should be as wide as possible and totally obtrusive. It is best that it have cushions so that it can double as a couch and therefore be quickly accessible. The apartment also does not need, but should have, an intimate table, bridge or otherwise, with two chairs intended for candlelit dinners that you may prepare.

You require a fully stocked liquor cabinet and a refrigerator that holds a six-pack of beer, one of club soda, one of coke, a container of milk, a container of orange juice, and some sliced cheese (individually wrapped). In the kitchen cabinet there should be a box of Ritz crackers, mustard, mayonnaise, a can of tuna fish, and various esoteric foods that will lie moldering that you bought on your first trip to the supermarket (snails, smoked oysters, Iranian caviar). You should also have on hand a can of peanuts and (compliments of Woolworth's) two knives, two forks, two spoons, a can opener, one dish towel (two if they are on sale), an ice tray, and a few highball glasses. It is always important that you pick up a couple dozen inexpensive bath towels. (Buy in quantity because you still will not have figured out the laundry procedures or the frequency or number of overnight guests.)

With the addition of blankets and sheets, your starter set is now complete. You are fully stocked, adequately staffed, and ready to go. (Incidentally, you might be able to make a deal with the superintendent's wife to clean the apartment once a week, preferably toward the weekend.)

Go, but where? During your divorce the friends of the

marriage have chosen sides. There are the friends that have picked the good guy's team, and there are those that have chosen the colors of the Bitch of Buchenwald.

From the latter expect nothing. As a matter of fact, you will never see them again except possibly at the weddings of your children.

This is good.

From the former, while you are still in stage 1 of rebaching and therefore an interesting topic of conversation (until somebody else gets divorced), you can anticipate receiving dinner invitations, at least one from each of these friends. Their wives will be intent upon feeding you good old-fashioned homemade chicken soup to help bind the wounds. Of course, they will also want to hear from you all of the latest developments in connection with your divorce. On some occasions, thought not as often as you would like, these wives will provide you with a female dinner partner whom you will be expected to "adore" or "find intellectually stimulating." She probably "just got a divorce herself" or "is a friend of the family or a college or business friend who happens to be around." Your reaction will be "I'm just not interested in that kind of thing right now, I really don't want to get involved." The horrible thing about that statement is that you may be believed.

At these dinners or other charming outings, you will find yourself effortlessly, and with great enjoyment, talking incessantly about your prior marriage—how sad you are, how you will never get married again, how you miss your children—and about various gory, and sometimes intimate, details concerning your divorce. At first, people will enjoy hearing your tale of woe. The second time around they will allow you to repeat all of what you said the first time. The third time around they will sit with glazed eyes. Unfortunately, there will be no fourth. You will then be relegated to telling the story of your marriage to anyone who will listen. Great listeners are taxicab drivers and bartenders; since you are picking up the tab, you can talk to your heart's content. Ultimately, even *you* will get bored with the sameness of the script.

Certainly your family will insist on having you over for dinner, even though during the divorce they compounded the problem with their supportive comments: "It couldn't happen to you two." "It's never happened in our family before." Or, if it has, "Not you, too. We thought you two were smarter than that." Or, "Mother and I have been through tough times together, but we have managed to stick it out. Why can't you?" Now they will provide a receptive ear for your misery. (Occasionally some misguided soul with reconciliation on the mind—or simply stupid—may invite you and your soon-to-be ex-wife to the same party. Do not go—you are not part of a Neil Simon or Noël Coward play.)

However, these dinner invitations—no matter how broad based and numerous your friendships and family may be—will dwindle down to a very few after the earliest days. By that time you will have received sufficient solace and really won't miss them. You will begin to learn how to feed yourself. Subject to your budget, you will eat out as often as possible, exclusive of breakfast. But for the most part, this will be feeding rather than dining, for there is nothing more intolerable than walking into a restaurant and eating alone. (Except trying to cook for yourself, and after having ruined assorted and sundry foods, having a stack of dirty dishes to contend with.) It is suggested that luncheon and dinner dates with business acquaintances be stepped up so that you can eat intelligently and well on expense accounts and settle for a hamburger at a fast-food restaurant when all else fails.

Along with an intelligent eating pattern, you should be able to develop productive drinking habits. Sitting alone at home staring at television is the loneliest thing in the world, and you really won't meet anybody in front of the tube. Find a friendly neighborhood bar with a friendly neighborhood bartender and cultivate him. If he is worth his tips, he will start introducing you to people. Even if they are not great people, you will at least have a sense of belonging in an uncomplicated and convenient place where you can sit with other warm bodies.

Laundry and cleaning are really pains in the ass. You have two alternatives and a compromise. You can send everything out to the laundry/cleaner around the corner, or you can send out shirts and use the laundry machines in the basement of the building or in the handy nearby laundromat for sheets and towels (and even you must remember not to mix whites with colors and not to put what goes in hot water in cold). While you do this, it will also occur to you to wonder what the hell is the sense of pressing sheets, pajamas, and underwear because they only get rumpled immediately anyhow. (One tip: it helps to fold them while they are still hot.) You can go to complete extremes and buy only wash-and-wear shirts. Until you have found a girlfriend willing to iron and sew (a rarity these days), remember that laundries also provide buttons and mend holes in socks. Socks with holes in them should probably be disposed of anyway, but unfortunately you can't do that with jackets lacking buttons.

Laundromats have one other great advantage. They are largely frequented by women. Hence, if you appear stupid enough about hot and cold temperatures (which should not be too hard), you'll have a great opportunity to meet females. Parenthetically, it should be noted that supermarkets carry the same advantage. Lasting romances have often started with casual check-out counter conversations or fender-bending supermarket cart collisions.

One enormous new problem looming in your life is your obligation to make heavy alimony and/or support payments. It matters little how reasonable the settlement was, for now that the negotiation has ended, you have been sunk to the status of debtor. From where you sit, it's like debtor forever without the benefit or salvation of bankruptcy. It is a debt that will be due on a fixed weekly or monthly date. It is a debt that you will never for a moment forget, but if you should for a moment forget, you have a creditor, unlike all other creditors, who will threaten you within a very short grace period. A landlord generally will not be upset if the rent payment is 15 days late. A bank generally will not bother you for 20 days or more if you are a mortgagor making a mortgage payment. If you owe American Express money, 30 or so days at least will go by before nasty notes arrive. The department stores give you some leeway and apologize a lot. However, with regard to your former wife the grace period starts the moment the mail is delivered on the day she would ordinarily expect the check, and extends through the time it takes her to walk from the mailbox to the telephone and dial her lawyer's number.

Nonpayment is a device for creating trouble and pressure. If for any reason you feel the need to create trouble and pressure, then withhold the money.

There is, however, a technique which, if properly employed, can save you money. Never make your payments on the same day. If the payments are due monthly, begin by making them around the first of the month. Do not indicate on the face of the check the month the check is intended to cover. As the year progresses, make the payment a little bit later in the month. Then occasionally skip a payment. In the beginning your ex-wife will notice this and complain. Apologize, indicate that you are broke (which is something you must always indicate), then make the payment. Eventually, if you have skipped enough payments and made enough partial payments ("adjusted" the following month), you should have successfully brought about total confusion, a confusion which your ex-wife's nonexistent book-keeping system will not be able to straighten out. If handled carefully, it is easy to avoid one or two months' alimony and support payments each year. You can even do better if your obligation to make payments is weekly. Obviously you are trapped when your payments are annual (camp, private school, orthodontia, etc.).

You must understand that even though part of the payment is a support payment, you are not drawing the check to the order of your children. The checks are being drawn to your ex-wife. She is merely putting the money in her bank account and using it as she sees fit. Do not feel, therefore, that you are cheating your children. If you sense that they are being short-changed, remember the secret signal, "you can always give more." All you are doing is beating the Bitch out of additional dollars that might go into *her* account.

·6·

Heirs and Heiresses Apparent

On the care, handling, and management of children there is much to be said, but in truth little to be done.

You will recall with clarity the real concern (perhaps your only honest emotion) that you felt for your kids when the time came to leave, the frequency with which you asked yourself what this would do to them. In retrospect, it is clear that it did very little to the children. As a matter of fact, they have survived better than anyone else involved in your divorce. But now you must do something.

When the separation agreement was still in draft form, specific visitation in all its complexity was unresolved, as were your rights. It was during this time that you made extraordinarily dramatic and unrelenting efforts to see your children. These efforts were frustrating. You fought with the Bitch about seeing them every weekend and on holidays, and made a dedicated effort to do so. As a result, you became a dedicated pain to them as well as to the rest of the world. Certainly you will recall the discussions that you had with your attorney regarding visitation rights. It was your position that you wanted to see them every weekend, on all holidays (legal or religious, and any others either not yet declared or somehow forgotten) and at such other times and dates that you felt were necessary for the happiness of Dick and Jane. Of course, what you were really feeling was a desire to be free of her and yet still maintain a father position, without having the kids on your neck all the time. At that time you were perfectly prepared to ignore the requirement that you let your ex-wife know when you would pick them up. It seemed perfectly reasonable just to drop in any old time. The compulsion here, in fact, was so great that you had little time left for anything else, except to fight with her when she appeared to resent your hanging around the house. It was quite a shock to discover that she did not accept lightly the idea of visitation rights taking place in her living room, even though it was once your living room and you still had title to the house. The change of a front door lock did give her psychological title and possession. You could no longer just hang around.

In truth, when that agreement was finally signed and you found your visitation strictly limited to perhaps every other weekend (and even then you had to let her know sufficiently in advance), it was then that your freedom really began. Finally you were able to enjoy weekends alone, but not too alone, with no obligation other than sensually to pamper yourself.

The attachment continues, however, and if she has not taken out her telephone or frustrated you by unlisting her number, you will probably find yourself calling Dick and Jane as often as every night. In the beginning the kids will be monosyllabic. The average conversation will go in one of two directions:

"How do you feel?"

"Fine."

Or, overheard in the background:

"I don't want to talk to Daddy now. I'm watching television."

These typical conversations will rarely change.

If your wife does acquire an unlisted phone number, go to court immediately and get that phone number. Dick and Jane need father's comfort. Father needs Dick and Jane (more). It is also imperative that your children have your phone number, even though they may call you at ungodly hours and in compromising situations. Give it to them anyway.

These phone conversations will be somewhat different. They will be more mercenary:

"I need . . ."

"How about my allowance?"

"Will you buy me . . ."

"My teacher says I have to have . . ."

"Can you get tickets for football, the World Series . . . ?"

Don't despair. It means they are thinking of you, even if only as the supplier of all good things. And you will, because you are good, provide allowances, and buy, and get, and give.

Frankly, telephone conversations with children are as boring to them as they are to you. Except for allowing you to stay in touch, they are fairly pointless.

Actual visitation, unfortunately, takes place in the same situation, but in a different house. (Same church, different pew.)

Under no circumstances should you expect your children to enjoy hanging around your apartment, particularly when they have left their toys, their friends, and a place much bigger than yours to come and visit you. On one occasion they will be overjoyed to be in your pad. The first time. Thereafter, if you want to maintain your sanity and have fun with them, keep them busy. Obvious suggestions include the circus, movies, amusement parks, football games, breakfast in, and lunch and dinner out.

In respect to eating out, if the children are under 12, find a restaurant with booths so that they can be trapped in the booth. Otherwise, the temptation for the kids to wander is too great.

If you want to maintain a glorious relationship with your kids, accept the fact that you have become a year-round Santa Claus, and no longer a disciplinarian. They will take advantage of this. Let them take advantage to whatever degree your sanity and your apartment furniture can bear. Let them do what they want. (Remember, it's crappy furniture anyhow.)

As the children get older their friends and surroundings at home will exert a greater pull than even you in your role of Santa. The solution to this problem, if it exists, is to invite them with their friends.

The only really worthwhile visitations that you will

have will occur during the summer. The thirty days with them that you have fought so hard for (if you can coordinate your summer vacation with theirs) are an opportunity to drop the role you assume during the other eleven months of the year and go back to being a father. You can only do this successfully if you have a place to take them to, a house in the country or at the shore, or some other place in a surrounding that they will really enjoy. Should you endeavor to keep them with you for thirty days in an apartment, you will not survive. They will hate you, and you will hate them.

There is a principle which you must early convey to your heir(s) and/or heiress(es). Your children have certain obligations and responsibilities to you. Just as you fulfill your obligations and responsibilities toward them by showing them you care and by spending time with them and money on them, so must they, in their own way, respond to you. Their response, however, must be learned; it is not automatic. They will learn to be responsible to you only if you clearly and repeatedly remind them to be so—and the sooner the better for you (and for all).

There is a time when children do not belong in your new life. You are entitled to, and must demand and receive, privacy. You must enjoy these moments without guilt. In other words, kids should, from time to time, be kicked out.

Children need limits when they are together with you, and even if you are going to be super easygoing, a nifty-keen, swell Daddy, you must also set basic ground rules (all of these subject to adjustment depending on age).

Baths (yes, with soap, without debate).

Bedtime (including conduct with babysitters and television turnoff times).

Meals (when and what to eat, who does the buying, who does the dishes afterwards, and who sweeps up crumbs on the living room floor in front of the television set).

Cleaning (stuff should be picked up unless it moves, without debate as to who dropped it; stepping over a motionless item is forbidden; beds must be acceptably made and rooms straightened up).

Answering the phone (and staying off it).

Home after dates (and where, and curfews, and if missed, phone calls).

Smoking (if, where, and where not). Grass (someplace else, and don't join in).

Liquor (beer, hard booze, if of age).

Sex (not here). Conversations regarding pills and masturbation. (Don't be afraid to handle it.)

Punishment (never corporal, never sadistic). Try to fit it to the crime.

Allowances. From five until about eight, 5 cents each birthday. Thereafter negotiate. Always pay it weekly. They will need money for junk and, more importantly, to buy you an occasional present.

In spite of the fact that you are sending the Bitch of Buchenwald inordinately high support and alimony money and are virtually destitute, she will, nevertheless, send the children to visit you in clothes that are either recycled Salvation Army or damn old. Their coats will be shabby, their socks full of holes, and, worst of all, none of their clothes will fit. Your choice here is either to take them to the nearest department store and buy them new clothes so that the world will not think you are a total shit, or to allow the world to think that you are a total shit. Go out and buy the clothes. However, under no circumstances are the children to return home with the new clothes. Send them back in the same shabby junk they arrived in, or else at the next visitation the shabby clothes will be back and you will never again see the good stuff you purchased. But don't believe that she is not buying them clothes: she could not, among her society of friends and family, exhibit the children in the discarded things in which you see them. She has purchased the clothes with the money from you which she is squirreling away. Never fear, Dick and Jane are not seen at school in last year's sneakers.

Her attitude is very simple. You have plenty of money, you are not sending her enough, she is barely getting by, and therefore *you* should buy the clothes. (Incidentally, she conveys this to the children, too, who in their own heart-rending manner will push for new clothes).

Diseases, cuts and bruises, broken bones, and other assorted maladies may frustrate many of your visitation plans. You will be told: "She can't come today, the doctors think it's cholera" or "He has been in bed all week with a cold, you wouldn't pick him up on a terrible day like today.''

Your answer, of course, is "Yes I would. I want my visitation.''

"That's fine for you to say, but you don't have to take care of them all week when they're sick."

If this stand-off continues, run, do not walk, to your attorney and fight for the visitation. Surreptitiously, whenever and wherever possible, your ex will attempt to undermine your visitations, even though publicly she will give lip service to the idea that your children need their father.

The children will arrive with complicated instructions for dealing with vitamin pills, allergy and cough medicine (how much to take and how many times), and bite plates (which must be worn, can't be lost and are). Don't be buffaloed. Use your own judgment. Don't rely on her or her doctor's opinion. Find a local pediatrician, and whenever the occasion arises, get a separate opinion.

In this situation and all others, act independently of your ex-wife with respect to your children.

A slightly more complex situation will arise when the children are away at camp or in a school play or graduating or are at the center of some function that mommies and daddies are expected to attend. This situation is probably more difficult for the children than anyone else. If Mommy has remarried, the child is stuck with the problem of introducing his mother (who has a different name), his stepfather (whom he may or may not be calling Daddy—which will drive you crazy), and his father. Simplicity is called for in a situation like this. Go alone. Don't sit near her. Make sure the kids know that you are there and leave. Hers is the homecourt advantage. Don't fight it. And don't chicken out. When the children are away at school or camp, it is wise to.let her go on visiting day; you go the day before or the day after. It is actually quite nice not having thousands of other parents crawling around.

A subject that certainly is near and dear to your own heart at this time is women. A most delicate subject no matter what the situation, it is particularly delicate with regard to your children.

The woman who has entered your life may, from time to time, press you to introduce her to your children so she can get to know them. After all, they are yours, she is good with children and can help you with them, and it is difficult for a man alone with young ones. Regardless of the "becauses," do not, under any circumstances, allow this meeting, casual or otherwise, to occur. This first woman (speaking now only of the first woman in your rebach life) may be seeking to establish herself firmly in your life, which is O.K. as a passing thing. But the minute you allow a contact with the rest of your family you have lent this relationship more permanence than you want it to have. Truly the temptation is great, for a woman's touch with the kids can be sensational, and her guidance can be helpful to them and to you. But it is equally true that to this woman (or to any woman thereafter) these children are part of the bounty. You are the main event, but she can't get you without them. The first woman you meet after the divorce may not be the woman who should meet your children.

The minute you introduce a woman to your children you have created a problem not only for yourself alone, but also a problem for you as the father of your children. They may adore her. She may be kind and sweet and do nice things for them, and soon they will want her around all the time. The temptation to make such an introduction is almost irresistible because in her role as playtime surrogate mother she occupies their time, leaving you less to worry about. They will not dislike her unless she is a complete dingaling. In that case, she probably won't want to meet your children anyway. The children will not resent the presence of another woman because by this time they will have accepted the fact that their mother and you are never going to make it; surprisingly, they, like married couples whom you meet, will be interested in seeing everything neat and tidy again. Simply translated, "Daddy needs a lady."

This situation is so bad as to be almost evil. It does the children no good to meet a series of women. You cannot be absolutely certain of the first woman, nor can you be absolutely certain of any woman who enters your life sooner than one year after your divorce is final (and not even then). Furthermore, all sexual activity must be eliminated when the children are around.

Since you have neither a woman who can act as part time mother, nor a bankroll that can stand constant depletion at circuses, movies, theaters, and restaurants, you must find friends with children whom you can visit. Your children can begin to build their own set of friends within your environment, and you can have friends on whom to dump the kids when the pressure in your apartment gets too great. The other side of this coin, of course, is that the people whom your children visit will feel perfectly free to dump theirs on you. Particularly good babysitters are other divorced men with children and relatives with children. A particularly bad babysitter to be resorted to only if you are in a "port in any storm" situation, is the divorced woman with children. Such an arrangement clearly carries with it certain overtones that exceed simply dumping kids. Handle this with the utmost caution, or you may find yourself with a brand-new, ready-made second marriage collection of offspring.

The need for comfortable survival with the kids is a matter on which a more practiced rebach can advise you, guide you, and counsel you well. Prior to their arrival, call the local magazine or newspaper that lists all the great children happenings for the week in your town. These happenings are usually inexpensive (if not free), long enough to be meaningful and entertaining, and sufficiently hazard-free to spare you from having to be concerned about the proximity of emergency medical aid or the police. These occasions are usually made more enjoyable if you are accompanied by another rebach father. Much can be learned from him. It is one of the best situations to learn by imitation. A father who has been at it for a while will know how to control children without either spoiling them rotten or turning himself into a case-hardened Mr. Hyde who will ruin the kids' afternoon.

What you are learning about children's special requirements such as clothes and toys is that children do not require lots of new things, but rather lots of things. Awful to have around are games with lots of little pieces. Pragmatically, however, they are dandy: you don't have to assemble them, and very quickly the little pieces get mixed together with other little pieces (or lost), and you never have to play the game with the children again. You may resign from the fray with the assurance that the children will develop their own games with the assortment of junk.

Parades, and there are great quantities of them for all sorts of illogical reasons, are a boon to your situation. You will learn quickly from other fathers (or from one bad experience) to arrive at a parade site early so that the kids can sit on the curbstone. Without such forethought, you will find the kids taking turns sitting on your shoulders. One child will happily view the parade while the other miserably tries to avoid being stepped on by the crowd. Also, your back will break. Unfortunately, on that basis you cannot remain at the parade site long enough to destroy many hours of the day. Parade planning is crucial.

If your children have reached the age of understanding, they should be turned on to one sort of athletic endeavor or another. Ice-skating, roller-skating, bicycle riding, and bowling are great day killers. If you have

not spent considerable time on ice skates or roller
skates, it is well to take a few lessons before you
undertake this adventure. Bone splints are dreadful.
They hurt like hell, and you cannot hold up a child while
suffering. If you happen to know a rebach father who is
a good ice skater, offer to take him and his children with
your children at your expense, provided he supervises
the skating so you can drink hot chocolate and ogle the
short-skirted females.

Hand holding, not a sport, must be done with tact and
dignity. To hold a little one's hand is not merely to put
your hand on his. You must also squeeze. The trouble is
that if you squeeze too hard, they holler, and if you
squeeze gently over a long period of time, your hand
will begin to feel like the frozen claw of a raven.

Bike riding is a good way to pass the time but best not
undertaken anywhere near hills. Coasting down is fun.
Peddling up is not. Halfway through you begin to think
of phrases like "cardiac arrest."

There are many techniques for teaching children how
to ride a bike. "Get on a bike and pedal while I run
behind you and hold the seat" is the most common. The
child spends some of his time pedaling, none of his time
steering, and most of his time looking over his shoulder
to make sure you are still holding on.

Teaching little kids to ride bikes goes like this:

1. Get a very small bike.
2. Take your small child and place him on the seat
of the very small bike.

3. Make sure his feet touch the ground on both sides (meaning the bike should not be tilted in either direction).

4. Find a very small hill.

5. Say to your child, "Let's see if you can lift your feet off the ground." After much persuasion, the child will lift his feet off the ground—and then put them back quickly to keep from falling.

6. Have him do this many times.

7. You are steadfastly holding the bike so it will not roll forward. Now you say to your small child, "Let's see how far forward you can roll without putting your feet down."

"No."

"Damn it, yes."

Because you are intellectually superior, you will eventually convince Dick or Jane that it is okay to let go.

8. Let go.

9. Say to the child, "Lift your feet."

10. The child lifts his feet and the bike rolls about an inch and a half.

11. The child puts his feet down.

12. The bike stops.

13. Slowly the child's confidence builds. Slowly the distance increases and he wants to try pedaling. However, there are two or three intermediate steps before that dramatic moment.

14. He is now coasting toward you and, unwise as it may seem, you put your hands out in front of you, spread your legs, allow the front of the bike to go between your legs, and catch the handle bars; he has

not yet learned how to stop. (If you feel timid, wear a steel cup.)

15. You now say, "Put your feet on the pedals but don't pedal."

16. He does so.

17. Now say, "We will practice stopping. Press the pedals backward." Eventually he does so. The bike stops, and he probably falls over. (Incidentally, always carry an available supply of Band-Aids for scratched knees.)

18. You have now reached the most dramatic moment in this creative period.

19. You say, "Pedal." He does. It is ghastly to watch. You say, "Stop." He does. It is ghastly to watch. Shortly thereafter, you have a full-fledged professional bike rider.

You have not only killed a day, but you have also developed a future day-killer. You have also placed on your back a brand-new financial burden known as "I need a new bike."

Advanced courses, such as 'feet up on the handle bars' or 'riding without hands,' will be learned by the kids themselves. The best thing you can do is not to watch. One special side benefit is the knowledge that when their mother sees them do this (and the first time she sees the kids covered with Band-Aids), she will die (figuratively, unfortunately).

Other useful means for killing visitation daytime hours include kite flying and fishing. Kite flying requires a kite; fishing requires a fishing pole and some water. Fishing absolutely does not require fish.

There is no underlying problem with kite flying once the kite is put together. If you buy a simple old-fashioned triangular type kite, you will appear to your child to be a genius as you put it together. However, the more elaborate geodesic-design kites will leave you looking like an utter moron. With either kite the trick is to get it into the air. It is best that you don't accomplish this too quickly; once the kite is flying, it really ceases to be very exciting for the children. Bored kids with a kite sailing two hundred feet above the ground are the same as bored kids anywhere else.

In connection with fishing, avoid a boat if possible, unless Dick and Jane can swim. The added complications of life jackets are extraordinarily aggravating while fishing.

Find a stream or bridge.

If possible, avoid catching fish. Under most circumstances this should be fairly simple. You cannot avoid using a hook because the kids will recognize fraud if you don't, but you can certainly use the wrong bait if you know what is running. The reason for this is simple. Your time should be spent untangling fishing lines and baiting hooks. You should not have the added problem of unhooking fish from a line that has managed to get itself tangled with everyone else's line. Also, you don't have to scale, gut, or cook an uncaught fish. There should be enough excitement in catching seaweed, crabs, and beer cans to keep the troops happy, and there will always be a handy assortment of rocks or other junk that the Izaak Waltons can throw, skip, or just dump in the water.

When planning more elaborate weekends, such as ski trips, or outings to the beach, you should keep in mind the traveling distance, the availability of counselors for the children during off-hours, and, least important, the snow or sun.

If there is someone else available to watch over the children on these weekends for any substantial length of time, you might conceivably be able to be alone and enjoy yourself. You are, after all, in a resort area.

Children are fun and great to have around, but, like rich pastry, they are best in limited quantities. The name of the game is planning. This is what is really meant by planned parenthood.

One final word. Should the relationship between you and your children collapse completely, you might do well to take yourself to a child psychologist or psychiatrist and discuss your problem. Because of your wife, it will undoubtedly be difficult to arrange for the children to visit these professional people. If your wife hasn't thought therapy necessary, she will blame the problem on you and suggest that *you* need a psychiatrist (which she will probably suggest every time she disagrees with you anyhow). Furthermore, she will insist on being party to the choice of the psychiatrist, and she will never get around to agreeing with your choice. If the latter becomes the problem, let her pick whomever she wants, so long as that individual is licensed to practice his profession. You still maintain a modicum of control. It's called payment. If you really dislike the therapist, you just stop paying. But if therapy is called for, your function will be solely to get your child there regularly.

·7·

The Alimony Erasure

He will appear innocently, as quietly as a thief in the night wearing tennis sneakers and walking on wet grass. The first indication of his arrival will be from your children.

"He took us to dinner."

"He brought us candy."

"His toys are crummy."

"Mommy sees him a lot."

"We visited his office."

"We met his ugly mother."

"He has a super car."

Then, finally, "He and Mommy are getting married."

Your heart will trumpet joyfully. Your mind will sing out, "No more alimony!" You will be pleased, excited, and only slightly disturbed that another man has moved into your house with your children. Naturally, you will wonder how this will affect them. One thing you can be certain of is that a new kind of aggravation has entered your life. You can be equally certain of two other things: first, that you are underestimating the size of that aggravation; and second, that if you are not already divorced, you are going to get that divorce jiffy-quick (upon your wife's insistence).

Incidentally, if the divorce for one reason or another has not yet occurred, this is the best possible time to re-evaluate your separation agreement and to make every effort to renegotiate it if you are not satisfied with what you signed. In such renegotiations she will accuse you of blackmail, or worse, and tell you that you are no good anyhow and you never were. When this attack begins, remember the famous childhood expression which has been passed on through the ages:

Sticks and stones may break my bones,

But names will never hurt me.

And, if it be blackmail, damn the torpedoes, and re-negotiate, and renegotiate.

Many of the things that took place between you and her before the arrival of this new man will fortunately fall by the wayside. No longer will she call you to discuss the multitude of problems that beset her. On the surface that had to do with children. In reality they dealt with her loneliness, her illnesses (rarely real), and even her boyfriends and her problems with them. She made every effort to maintain a relationship with you, even though she was vicious and dirty during your separation and took too damn much money from you. All of this was ignored repeatedly. Interestingly enough, these calls generally took place after 2 o'clock in the morning (the lonely hours begin then), and frequently hidden in them was the suggestion that you take her out to dinner or on a date to better resolve the problems. Underlying

all was an absolutely clear-cut sexual proposition, re-
vealed in statements like:

"If nothing else, we used to make great love and I bet
we still can."

"Let's go to bed with each other and see if anything is
left, at least in that area."

Certainly you didn't seriously consider any of the
propositions. Nor did you consider the fact that she
really needed your advice—and even took it. You didn't
consider any of this because your dislike for her was
enormous. It was impossible for you even to contemplate being so horny that you could ever put your act
together sufficiently to gain an erection for her. Now all
of this exasperating contact has ended with the arrival of
her new choice. He is the man of her hour, a new
recipient of her complaints and frustrations, and your
heaven-sent bearer of relief from alimony.

You will also recall that the problems that had developed with your visitation impelled you occasionally
to write letters to her. The form of these letters varied
little. You demanded only your rights and expressed in
certain key phrases your gross indignation.

"I intend to pick up my children according to the
agreement. If you intend to cause problems, I would
appreciate knowing in advance to avoid embarrass-
ment."

"Whether or not the children go to camp is entirely
secondary to my rights of visitation."

"I am indeed shocked by the attitude you expressed
over the telephone to me."

"You are interfering, thwarting, and frustrating the father-child relationship which is so important to the maturity of my children."

"Your statement that you are helping the children understand me is lip service. I don't need your help."

"I will not permit you to interfere with visitation on my birthday."

"Your lack of sensitivity is appalling."

In the past, these letters were followed by incensed telephone attacks. Your response over the phone, though initially subdued and rational even in the face of her fish-mongering, escalated to shouting. Be happy with the knowledge that you are past this.

Your well-thought-out letters will now be responded to with equally well-thought-out letters which he will write but she will sign. God help you if he is a lawyer because there is nothing he would rather do than prove to her just how good a lawyer he is, and he will prove it with your blood. (Obviously she will not need to pay legal fees and, just as obviously, you will need to pay your lawyer.)

The first time you hear your children refer to him as "Daddy" you will split a gut. You will grab your separation agreement, only to find that there is nothing in it about this. Then you will call your lawyer and ask him what you can do. Finally, you will become unreasonable. Your first reaction with the children will be to say, "*I* am your father and the *only* father you will ever have." The kids will not fully understand, and you will eventually find that the best thing is just to leave it alone. If they are calling both of you "Daddy," forget it, keeping in mind that by the time they are twenty-one they will have figured out where all the pieces go. In the meantime, it doesn't make any difference.

And it really does not.

He will assume certain prerogatives in and around your ex-house. If you are reasonable, you will be able to see things from his point of view.

Don't be reasonable.

He will discipline the children. If at any time you find that he is hitting the children, tell him to lay off. If he refuses, and if he is smaller than you, tell him you will break his neck. If he is bigger, tell him you will hire somebody to break his neck. If he is not responsive to either threat, go into court for some form of order protecting them from this "wild man." You really don't want anyone spanking your children other than the Bitch of Buchenwald, if she finds it necessary. As far as you are concerned, he has not been appointed or elected a father. He is nothing more than a man living in the household with your children.

It won't work that way, but maintain that hard-nosed position.

Do not, under any circumstances, seek to make a friend out of this man. Do not seek his advice on how to handle *her*. Do not discuss with him the problems of your children or ask his opinion. He is an adversary. He cannot be expected to be sane or reasonable because he married *her*. At best he will only spit the balls that she will make. At worst, if you let him in, he will make a few himself. If you allow him to cope with the problems of your children, you have given him authority that he could not otherwise achieve. Until he is willing to assume financial responsibility for the children, and until you are willing to allow him to do this, his position in that household with respect to the children can only be as secure as you permit it to be.

Don't!

Very likely your ex-wife will have, for one reason or another, worked out a bad second marriage. If that should be the case and she seeks your advice, you will be smart enough to keep your hands off.

Your children will recognize quickly that a new dimension has been added to the conflict which previously existed solely between you and your ex-wife. Because they are smart, they will take advantage of the situation in the most devious ways. They will enjoy relating to you all the rotten, immoral, and dishonest things that the new husband is doing. They will also continue to tell you about all the rotten, immoral, and dishonest things that their mother is doing. You can either encourage this, which is fun, or ignore it. It is best to discourage it. Just as they are talking about him and her with you, you know they are also talking about you with him and her. Whenever possible, say unkind things about your ex-wife and her husband. Challenge and hold up to ridicule their overall lifestyle, always making it clear (as humbly as possible) that the way you live is the proper way. Remember, you are the good guy.

It is imperative that while the children are young, you

create the image of yourself as Mr. Clean. This ploy is more important than attempting to create negative pictures of their mother and stepfather (don't you love that word?).

No matter how tempting the opportunity, never destroy this man totally. It is fine to belittle him in a limited way, to denigrate him modestly, to demean him whenever appropriate, to chip at his edges (and to enjoy it), but under no circumstances should you destroy him in his entirety. It is in your best interest that he marry your ex-wife. The marriage between the two of them (hopefully they will deserve each other) should beautifully eliminate all of your alimony obligations. This is manna from heaven, and this match must be treated as if it were made in heaven until it is legally consummated. Thereafter, any gentleness you may have felt a need to show him, as well as any understanding toward your wife's new matrimonial relationship, can be discarded, and you can be as destructive as you feel the need to be.

Depending on the ages of the children and your relationship with them, it is possible that they will desire to live with you. If they are very young, this desire will be due in part to the fact that you play Santa Claus. They may also be annoyed at their stepfather for trying to be a surrogate father. It is best for their sake that you do not create in their minds the idea that moving in with you is possible, for until they are old enough to express their wishes it is not possible. This delay can create much frustration. (For children an hour is a day, a day a month. Time is a different dimension.)

. THE LION'S SHARE .

Your children will eventually reach an age of consent (the age at which a child can logically defend what he is doing; depending on the child, it can begin as early as ten or eleven years). They must know now that all they have to do to live with you, assuming you want them, is to move out and move in. Once they have physically detached themselves from their mother's house and moved into yours, it will be extremely difficult for anyone to budge them.

The possibility of the children moving in with you gives rise to great personal ego satisfaction. "I'm a better mother than she is a father." "She deserves it." However, this apparent victory must be recognized as possibly Pyrrhic.

A bachelor's household with children is no longer a bachelor's household. It is almost unnecessary to say (but should be said) that full-time living together cannot in any sense be compared to the simplicity of visitation. It will only work if the child is very strong and confident, has very positive feelings toward you, and is totally misunderstood at home.

·8·

Dear Abby—I Need You— Where Have You Gone?

It's a fear that starts the day you first consider the possibility that you might be single again. It becomes progressively greater as your inclination to leave grows stronger. When you finally do make a break, suddenly you must face it: You are alone.

There is very little you can be told about loneliness. It's like the first time you had a fight or stepped into a boxing ring. It makes very little difference how many people are standing on the sideline assuring you they're behind you. It makes very little difference how many people have told you you have nothing to fear, for, in fact, when you are in the ring you're very much alone. It is a new feeling, and you have every reason to be very much afraid. There is no such thing as getting used to loneliness, for a lonely feeling can never be said to be better than before or partially better. It's like trying to say partially dying or slightly dying.

When you are lonely, you are lonely.

The forces of loneliness, however, can be challenged in practical, pragmatic ways. The antidote to loneliness has become a product. It is packaged and sold just like Crest toothpaste or Coke.

The newspaper classified sections carry advertisements:

"S.W.O.R.D.—Single, Widowed, or Divorced. Call (telephone number)."

"A totally new lifestyle for single people . . . Best of all, intelligent conversation. For information, write (address)."

"Divorced or Separated? Share and learn with others in coed groups, limited size. For further details call (telephone number)."

"Charlie's & Sarah's. We don't promise a great time. We'll provide the cozy atmosphere and music, the rest is up to you. Casual dress."

"Liberate your spirit with sensitive, caring people in a setting of elegance and natural beauty. Music, yoga, singles. All ages."

"Huge Eastside party. Bright, open, and aware. Come meet lots of interesting singles. Free wine and music. Call (telephone number)."

"Single again? For the formerly married of mid-years, the Universalist Church brings you a rap session for those who would like to begin anew. A party precedes and follows the rap session. Bring new people into your life."

But the classifieds are rarely the answer. Most of the people whom you will meet in these groups are in exactly the same situation as you. They are lonely and miserable and talk nonstop about their previous marriages, their children, and their particular "Bitch of Buchenwald." They are not uplifting. But groups do provide an opportunity to meet women. Many of these women, you will discover, are somewhat long in the tooth, have been in the groups too long, and are there only in the hope of meeting a man. The right ones can provide adequate sexual companionship, but between sexual encounters there is a good deal of time in which you must talk, which is unfortunate, and listen, which can be worse. The conversations are usually based on loneliness and misery.

These groups are not proper group therapy sessions and should not be approached with that thought in mind. It is sufficient to say that if the loneliness becomes too bad, a warm body is the best antidote.

You may find a slight satisfaction in the thought that if you are lonely, certainly your ex-wife is equally lonely. You may find satisfaction in that thought if in fact it is true, but probably it is not.

Consider the following. You left your former home. You left *her* with most of *your* possessions, with your children, and in surroundings that she had long been used to. Thus, it is unlikely that she will feel quite the same loneliness that you feel.

When you sit in your first trashy apartment and reach for a book that is in fact in your former bookcase, the twinge you feel is a twinge of loneliness. The possessions you took with you (your clothes and the hi-fi set) are not the kind that will give you feelings of warmth. The things that you were truly comfortable with you probably left behind. She, on the other hand, still has those things that make her feel at home. What she may from time to time describe to her friends as loneliness is more likely just boredom.

Unless you are aggressively fighting your loneliness, you will suffer inner doubts about yourself, inner doubts stemming from having too much time to think. Your thoughts will run amuck.

"Who am I?"

"What am I?"

"What have I accomplished?"

"What have I failed to accomplish?"

"There is no meaning to my life."

"There is no meaning to a single man's life."

"What's the meaning of it all?"

"What's the difference?"

"There is no such thing as love."

Be assured, you will get used to being alone. The loss of old possessions will lose significance as you acquire new ones.

You will not have to worry about your self-image because during this period your self-image will change from month to month, perhaps even from day to day. Though in the beginning you will find it hard to think in terms of being a bachelor, you will ultimately find it difficult to think in terms of ever being married.

In the beginning you will find solace in the role of the man standing alone against the world. But even this will change, without your noticing it happening.

The days you will feel sorriest for yourself will be December 24 and 25, December 31 and January 1. These are the best days for feeling lousy. There are, of course, other holidays that will be distressingly lonely. Thanksgiving is a pip. It's a pip whether you like turkey or not. Ultimately, you will attempt to treat holidays as just ordinary days. You will not be successful, and so you will eventually learn to make plans for these occasions to counteract your loneliness.

The best plan is not to leave your wife earlier than January 2. If you can work it out, January 2 is exactly the day you leave. Even though you may feel that there can be nothing more depressing than being with somebody you dislike during these special holidays, it won't be so bad because there will usually be other people around celebrating the holidays with you. If you have already left your wife, be certain that on these four days you are totally occupied, even if you choose these dates for a blind, smashing drunk.

On your birthday, if your children are too young to remember and their mother did not remind them, it can be the pits.

Certainly if you have already stumbled into your first grand passion, you need no longer worry about loneliness. But until you find that grand passion, you will reel a lot.

Become active. Play tennis. Ski. Jog. Collect stamps. Play bridge or backgammon.

If you do any of these things well, continue, but also pursue something that you have never pursued before. If you play tennis, learn backgammon. If you jog, join a stamp club. If you play bridge, learn to ski. In other words, get involved. (The danger, of course, is that you

may get overly involved in too many activities.) Start
slowly, and you will begin to meet people. At first,
people are warm bodies; if you try hard enough, they
eventually become friends. One of these friends might
be a woman.

There are places you can go that package loneliness,
but on a higher level; for example, a major hotel that has
set aside a singles weekend, with enough facilities to
keep you busy even if you are not attracted to any of the
singles. If the hotel is big enough, the confusion and
noise should be on a grand scale, and loneliness is not
possible in such a surrounding. Airlines and steamship
lines also cash in on this disease. Quite frankly, the only
bed partner that loneliness will embrace is you alone.

The final solution to loneliness is a large surrounding
of male friends who will fill in comfortably when you
are not in hot pursuit of some lucky female.

A word at this point about the value of psychiatry,
psychology, and/or group therapy. Therapy can become the first line of defense against loneliness and its
handmaiden, anxiety.

There is undeniable value to psychological or
psychiatric therapy. There are two considerations. The
first, a practical matter, is the dollars you have to spend.
If you have the money, the second and most important
consideration is the psychiatrist or psychologist himself. You will find that the right psychiatrist or
psychologist for you is not necessarily the person who
was right for your best friend or your favorite second
cousin. If you decide to embark on this course, it is

essential that you do not make a commitment to any professional person until you have satisfied yourself that you are comfortable with him (or her). The best psychiatrist or psychologist may for one reason or another be wrong for you. In your situation, a female psychiatrist or psychologist may be better for you than a male. The insights you come away with may be a little different, and that difference may be of tremendous value.

If you cannot afford private sessions on a regular basis, a group session in the hands of a trained person can be invaluable. A word of caution: a group run by an untrained or lay individual can be destructive.

There is no question that in the early stages of your divorce psychiatry is at least as important as a good attorney. It may well save you considerable pain, much of which will fall under the general heading of loneliness. But do not think that these professionals can save your marriage. They are not masons; they do not have the mortar to rebuild a marriage. Conceivably they can save you from making the same mistakes again.

Group therapy is an unusual experience. A group can be terribly supportive. It raises hell with your ego, attacking your lies, challenging your male chauvinism. After the group has done its worst, it tells you how good you are. A group will manhandle your sex problems, your father problems, your mother problems, your big brother problems, your business problems, and, when you lash out, your temper. While this is going on, you will be doing the same number on someone else, and after a while group will become a very useful crutch in a period when you need a useful crutch. A professionally run group will be bound to the principle of confidentiality and will not permit uncalled-for expressions of aggression, hostility, or scapegoating toward any member. Eventually, however, you will outgrow the group and leave it, just as others in the group have done previously.

The group is an asexual body, and female contacts that you make there are best treated as aunts or sisters. To cross that very fine line is to create an impossible relationship similar to the relationship between a python and a rabbit. The group will be unforgiving, and the woman won't be any good in bed. Surprisingly enough, you may be even worse in bed than she.

The dynamics of a group should be such that in each of its individual members you are able to see a caricature of part of yourself.

Anxiety and loneliness are frequently the major common denominator in a group. (These emotions run you up and down like a yo-yo.)

The language of the group can be harsh when directed at you, but you need the attack to cleanse your mind. You will survive.

"Why should you have little problems when you can create a holocaust?"

"You're the kind of guy that sometimes walks past a mirror and expects to see nothing."

"You stinking death junkie."

"Don't be upset because somebody thinks that

you're stupid or someone thinks that you're a schmuck, but rather ask yourself why you are a schmuck. Why are you stupid?''

"You are shoveling shit against the tide.''

"What makes you think things have to be fair? Whoever made that rule?''

"You want to be right and liked . . . get over it.''

"It's time to do—not to be done to.''

When this attack is over, even though you may be totally committed to the group, you cannot help wondering why. Sometimes when you're up to your ass in alligators, you forget why you wanted to drain the swamp.

If you've forgotten, remember that you need the group to kill the pain. However, as in setting a broken arm, the pain is necessary to insure the cure.

·9·

Love's Lending Library

"I've never paid for it."

"There's enough around for me to get all I want for free."

"There are several things that can happen with one of them, and none of them are good."

"Who needs it?"

The above is a lot of crap. Hookers, whores, prostitutes—whatever you want to call them—serve a marvelous function. Properly handled, a relationship with a prostitute can protect you from becoming overly involved with other females. First of all, they are females. Second, they are emotional without emotion. Third, they are convenient and present no complications. There is nothing more satisfying, when immediate stress requires it, than your friendly hometown hooker. There is only one problem: they cost. But the cost is not necessarily in direct proportion to the skill. Some are intelligent. For some, their service is an avocation. Most have reasonably nice faces and figures. Frankly, a well-handled professional fuck can be as satisfying as an amateurish coquettish schlep to bed with a female who has cost you drinks, dinner, and theater, and who,

LOVE'S LENDING LIBRARY

when you finally get to her bed, destroys the game with her complex female rules and regulations. Her rules and regulations, which you've heard a thousand times before, eliminate all spontaneity.

"I don't do that."

"You make me feel like an animal."

"You're too rough."

"I've never done this before."

"That's all you're interested in."

"Tell me you're in love with me."

You struggle to help this uptight female achieve orgasm, though even a stick of dynamite could not accomplish that result. This is not the way it is with all women, but certainly it is never this way with a hooker. There *can* be great female relationships. As for the sexual side of a great female relationship, you should look for a woman with the in-bed abilities of a professional.

There are two kinds of prostitutes. The first is the street-walker sponsored by a pimp. Her sole desire is to knock you off as quickly as possible, and with her you run a substantial risk of contracting major disease for which there is no known vaccine or cure, i.e., fractured skull, slashed face, or dead-on-arrival. The second and more comfortable type is the classic call girl. From this woman you can usually expect a comfortable apartment or some other place where you can relax and feel secure. She will be a professional listener who will nod approval or disapproval at the right moments during your soliloquy. She will even, in a non-smart-ass way, reply to your idiotic question, "How did you get into this?"

. THE LION'S SHARE .

This kind of female, similar in many respects to the American idea of a Japanese geisha, ain't all that bad.

Meeting ladies of the night can be somewhat complex. Other single, divorced, or widowed men may indicate where they are and arrange an introduction. A married friend who is miserable at home may even more readily provide you with that information.

The price is generally non-negotiable when the standard services are requested, and negotiable when you ask for something more exotic or requiring a longer time. A basic ground rule, however, with this kind of relationship is to establish the price clearly in the beginning. Even with the classic call girl, you are liable to be ripped off if the price isn't understood from the start. There are other ground rules which should be observed. When you have been storing up energy, you may find one orgasm barely sufficient. There are some hookers who charge by the hour. There are others who base their charge on the number of times you come. Since they refuse checks and credit cards, cost should be determined early and quickly.

The best single feature of this professional-client relationship is obviously the girls' bedside manners. They await you eagerly, admire your studlike qualities, are without qualms with regard to any sexual act, appear to enjoy themselves immensely, and treat you fondly.

You need only get past the hang-ups of your ego. A prostitute can save enormous wear and tear on your head and enormous energy wasted on females who aren't worth the effort (as a result, you may even save money).

You don't have to please her, and she doesn't have to like you. Besides, she will make you feel that she *does* like you and that you *have* pleased her.

The first time you go to a whore you will be nervous and timid for any number of reasons. The second time will be easier and not necessarily with the same one. The third time it's a piece of cake.

There is little difference between paying cash for services rendered and buying dinner, gifts and flowers, and making loans that will never be repaid.

Even if you are especially particular about whom you take to bed and frequently find that you can't have an erection with just any woman, you should try a hooker. "How can I make love to a hooker when I need to have a relationship with a woman to make love at all?" is a question you needn't entertain. The joy in being with a hooker is that you can fantasize anything you like and know that your fantasies will probably come true. The fact is that you can be totally selfish and not do a damn thing and simply enjoy everything that is going to happen and does happen. In short, you don't even have to make love; you get made love to. There is no macho involved. There is no stud ability to be challenged. It is simply sex for recreation—if not sex at its best, at least sex at its most convenient. It is virtually impossible to be turned off by a good hooker.

Hookers usually live alone, except for the super madams like Xaviera Hollander who have large stables.

You should be forewarned that even the sweetest hooker will not for one second accept being cheated. If you don't have the money to pay for the pleasure, don't go. Her reaction to your failure to pay can be more violent than anything you have ever experienced, and you can easily get hurt. Single professional girls are quite capable of inflicting enormous bodily harm by way of pots, knives, vases, and huge dogs. It is not a time to play smart-ass.

It is not unusual to find two prostitutes working together. In such a circumstance, you may think:

"What a marvelous time I'll have with two of them."

"They'll perform great sexual gymnastics."

"They'll perform great sexual gymnastics on each other for my benefit."

Avoid this kind of thing. First, it will cost you twice as much. Second, when they start on you it will turn into sheer confusion. There will be just too many breasts, too many hands, too many vaginas—and one pathetic penis. (This is one situation in which your penis may become totally disoriented.)

If you think that you would like to be a voyeur and observe the two of them together, be forewarned that, more than likely, the performance will be staged, disappointingly so, and that you will be stuck with the choice of picking one of them just to have an orgasm so you can get the hell out. (It is highly unlikely that two females who are selling themselves to men will also have genuine lesbian qualities and be eager to demonstrate them to a buyer like you.)

Don't assume that all of your fantasies will be acceptable to every hooker. The fantasies that you most enjoy are probably second nature to the average professional. However, you may have some way-out thoughts that are best broached tentatively and mentioned to the pro beforehand. By way of example, there are literally no limits to any sort of oral or anal intercourse, but if you happen to have the bright idea of tying someone up, it is suggested that the watchword be caution.

The only taboo that exists in connection with a pro is involvement. Remember, she is an extremely wise woman; she has been exposed to all sorts of "Charlie Brown crazies" and has learned how to handle men. So, as miserable as you may be feeling and as sympathetic as she may appear—and even if you see one particular woman so often that you think you really know her— don't allow her into your straight, normal, average life. *Do not*:

1. Take her to lunch
2. Loan her money
3. Buy her presents
4. Invite her to your apartment
5. Introduce her to your friends other than as a professional
6. Take her home to mother for chicken soup
7. Help her out of trouble of any kind. If she gets busted, don't find her a lawyer. (She no doubt retains a couple already.)

The problem with turning this business relationship into something more is a major one. In bringing her into your life, giving her your home phone number, you may conceivably be inviting violence in the form of black-mail. Even if you are not married, depending upon your business and personal life, you may be badly embarrassed. By way of example, a subtle remark like, "I have an agent who thinks I ought to write a book about the men I've known," is at best a subtle form of blackmail. You are wise to respond with great encouragement and to say that you will be one of the first to buy the book. Certainly under no circumstances do you ask, "Are you using names and is mine one of them?" The answer to that question you can guess. A milder form of nuisance bred by an overly cozy relationship is having the woman constantly on your hands with—because of the nature of her profession—her great or minor problems. All will be original, some trivial, some incomprehensible, but, once again, some of them will be downright dangerous.

If you become a buddy of a hooker, you're opening the door on the tiger, not the lady.

Occasionally, incredible as it may seem, you may feel that you can reform a hooker, or that you have fallen in love with a hooker and that this emotional involvement is deep and meaningful. Should that occur, book a session with the best psychiatrist you can find.

Though throughout your newly acquired bachelor life you should in all sexual relationships maintain the position of the "fuckor," there is one occasion when you should willingly relinquish this role. With a hooker, you are a "trick." You are getting fucked. The relationship

itself is meaningful solely because you are without obligation to function at any level. You should be agreeably satisfied if the job done on you is workmanlike, and workmanlike means that you have had a hell of a good time. Of course, if you are not satisfied, there is no money-back guarantee.

Having recognized that this relationship is wholly physical and that your commitment to it is nonexistent, your enjoyment of it should be total.

Enjoy being fucked! This is the only time it's fun.

It is hardly likely that you will ever find a straight woman who can assume the role of a hooker. This is the fantasy of the woman who wishes to think of herself as "total" (from the book of the same name). Professional fucking does not really mix with housekeeping, raising children, and a career. It is probably true that many women make an effort in that direction, and some of them even believe that they are that accomplished. Though some women do more than just lie spread-eagled, they still can't compare.

The hooker will never say, "You screwed up; however, please keep trying until you get it right." The amateur, directly or indirectly, will. It cannot be otherwise.

·10·

Corporate Reorganization

Successful organized rebaching (as opposed to the disorderly scramble that your life has become) begins with the group.

Somehow, somewhere, in some fashion, you will meet another divorcing male, and then another, and then a third, and so on. Eventually some of them will become friends, and once having developed male friendships, you are on your way to total rebach growth. No longer are you obliged to feed a female merely in order to have company (as opposed to feeding in order to fuck), but rather you are in a position to enjoy simple things at half the cost—and not alone.

More importantly, the divorced male you meet can introduce you to many of life's subtleties: where the action is; parties; vacations; showgirls; joint outings with your kids and his; advice, good or bad; guidance, good or bad; counseling, good or bad; private clubs; hookers; charge accounts; eating, drinking, and women; better working habits; summer houses.

Other divorced males are the key to your lifestyle. Imitate them, until you have developed a style of your own.

. CORPORATE REORGANIZATION .

"Where the action is" is a phrase which means many things, for example, an introduction to a friendly swinging bar. This is easily accomplished by a male friend who is known there. The pain of walking alone into a bar and staring at a mirror is gone. The clumsiness which the early stage of divorce brings with it in meeting new females disappears when you are with a friend who has been at it for a while. It is like an open invitation, and after a while you won't need to go with someone in order to be comfortable because you will know many people who, as a clique, spend time in the same bar.

"Where the action is" can also mean any number of summer or winter resorts. At best difficult to handle alone, these are a cinch if you are with a male friend who has been there before.

In all cases of "where the action is," a personal style must be developed so that the anxiety generated by single men and women all eyeing each other does not become overwhelming. In the beginning this style may be imitative (your own radar may be slow to develop), but at least you are out of the shell. Eventually the confidence you have lacked because of your age, height, size, color, weight, or previous condition of servitude will return sufficiently so that every man you look at and compete against does not appear to be Robert Redford, Arnold Schwarzenegger or Roger Staubach, but rather just another slob. To properly round out this style, you should cultivate a number of divorcing males.

Aside from the nightclub, bar, or summer or winter resort, "where the action is" might also mean parties. These, inordinate in number, are most frequently given by lonely females who invite other lonely females and who always welcome a new male simply because he is untried, untested, and unknown and for that reason has great potential as boyfriend, lover, or (heaven help you) husband. In the beginning, at these parties you can expect enormous attention, far more than what your appearance, personality, or other attributes may entitle you to. This is simply because these women would like to protect you from the horror of "professional" singleness that your other male friends have fallen into. But realize with caution that, just as you are being introduced by professional divorced males, you are being introduced to women who are equally professional at looking for a man. All protestations to the contrary, most of these women are dedicated to entrapping you.

Regrettably, these kinds of parties do not bring out the best of the female species. Those really attractive, in mind as well as in face and body, are well bedded elsewhere and don't need you.

Nevertheless, the experience is worthwhile. The potential is greatly limited, but there is always the off chance of some less stagnant female arriving and the equally slight possibility that you will be able to outmaneuver your male friends and get close to her. This kind of party is merely a way station and will soon be only an occasional fond memory.

As your rebach group develops, and as you are introduced to the more sophisticated divorced males, you will eventually go to male rebach parties. In order for these parties to be successful, one member of your group must have connections with a large assortment of women. The most successful of these parties are given by a man whose contacts are on a professional level (professional and theatrical people). If you become involved in such a circle, the parties are at worst interesting and at best out-of-sight. A well-run party will include the female chorus of whatever show may be running at that time (arriving late), unemployed actresses (arriving early), and the line from the late show at the local nightclub. Include in that last category late-working Bunnies, if there is a local Playboy Club. These girls come not for food, and not for just any men, but rather because they believe that the men there have money (and are available), have position and power (and are available), have contacts (and are available). They are there as users, and they will accept most graciously your help with their careers without particularly caring if you are not yet divorced. To them, available merely means willing to help. These girls are usually beautiful, hypertense, and intellectually stimulating. They are no less eager than the long-time female singles, but their eagerness is easier to take, at least for a while.

Be assured that underneath it all they will be tough, for their survival depends not necessarily on talent alone, but also on having a man to support them intellectually, and sure as hell financially. Here you must go by the advice of your more experienced, wiser male friends.

The true lifestyle renaissance does not begin until you have, with your male friends, rented or otherwise acquired a summer or winter house away from your town. At that point you adopt a brand-new identity, for you have achieved the status of a grouper.

You will find that many real estate agents and house-owners will not rent to groupers. Groupers are known as wild, dirty, sexually perverted, and unpleasant to have around. You will also discover that when you indicate a willingness to pay outrageously for crummy accommodations, you will be much more acceptable. Even if you have enough money to rent this accommodation by yourself, you will be suspect because you are not dragging with you a wife. If you have the needed funds and are, in fact, inclined to rent alone, you should not because ''where the action is'' is where the bodies are. You cannot by yourself produce a sufficient number of bodies, and your male friends will not be around enough of the time to people a summer or winter house.

The best vacation house-hunters (and the best year-round apartment- or house-hunters) will be female real estate saleswomen or brokers. They will, relentlessly and in the face of all discouragement, dedicate themselves to finding you a home, not merely shelter. This has very little to do with their professional competence, but rather with the instinctive female homing urge (that is, make a home for a male). Their male counterparts have no such philosophical bent. The female cannot help being a home-finder, whether for a month, for a vacation, for a year, or forever.

This area of the real estate business (apartment and house rentals or sales) is a haven for the single or recently divorced female who is without direction and who has decided that she needs a career. She has discovered a career—or so she thinks.

The house rules for the group rental should be fairly simple. Each of you antes up dough, someone buys the liquor and whatever food is required and someone pays all the bills. When the money runs out, everyone antes up some more.

With respect to women, there is no obligation for everyone to produce his own. Hopefully, the members of the group, if it is a decent group, will work together to fill the house on a one-for-one basis and will change the female bodies, preferably three or four times, during the winter or summer season. Depending on the size of the group, at least one male will have a girlfriend, and she will be around through most of the vacation. Appoint her housemother and let her delegate the various chores to various females on each weekend. Someone must cook, someone must clean, someone must make beds, someone must wash dishes. The way the women react to their assigned chores will also tell you a lot about them. (Incidentally, the house should be big enough so that each member of the group has his own private bedroom.)

Girls who are new to this kind of scene may at first feel awkward about going to bed with you with everyone else suspecting that this may be the first time. A good housemother can make a discreet speech, the sense of which is that the weekend guests are not at a Girl Scout camp.

There is no question that with a plethora of women tripping through the house you will find yourself attracted to someone. The following is a cardinal rule that must never be violated (under any circumstances): you must never, repeat *never*, go out with another male friend's girlfriend. This is the Achilles heel of any functioning group. There is no possible way you can properly ask a friend for permission. Even if it appears that the relationship that existed between your friend and his girlfriend has ended, this female must be avoided like the plague. Under no circumstances should you compete either openly or surreptitiously with a male friend in your group. Having joined the group, you must accept the principle that all women can be duplicated. You can find someone else. It is interesting to note that, as harsh a rule as this may appear to be, men will not usually violate it. Women, though, have no such compunction. If a woman decides she wants a man, she will seek him out, climb over her friends to get to him, and justify easily all her maneuvers.

There is no room for this in the society of divorcing males.

The advice, guidance, and counseling available from other divorcing males will unquestionably influence your life in many other areas.

In the first place, there is your business. Your self-discipline in your professional life has undoubtedly suffered badly and will need a total overhauling. Frequently, however, you are in a situation where you cannot see the forest for the trees.

Your rebach friends can.

They will, by example if not by direct comment, lead you down the path of righteousness and strength and turn you back into a fully functioning business executive. You will learn that having female friends call you during your office hours, though satisfying to the ego, is enormously destructive to the thinking process. It is also time-consuming, for rare is the woman who says, "I only called to say hello," who really only called to say hello. Similarly, "I only called to see how you were feeling" does not mean she only called to see how you were feeling. And you are a damn fool if you believe that you can end that comment with a simple "Fine." Unfortunately, in the early days you will have made your number readily available and you will be required to spend considerable time saying "Hello" and "Fine."

No matter what your business or profession, the same females who phone will find occasion to visit you at your office to discuss their professional problems, especially if you are a lawyer, doctor, or accountant. This has two major drawbacks. First, their problems will generally be invented, and if they are real, more than likely of such small consequence that it would be embarrassing for you to make short shrift of them. The inevitable result is valuable time spent on a valueless cause. You won't even be paid for your advice. Having been through this before, your friendly rebach advisor will point out to you how misdirected your compassion can be.

It is never difficult to say to a woman that you would rather not have her call or visit you at the office. It requires only that you fabricate extraordinary pressures and enormous demands on your time; tell her that you have to accomplish in eight hours what any other human being would normally expect to do in thirty-two. If she doesn't get the message, you have painted the picture badly, or she is a dolt.

Your hours have become somewhat erratic. This is partly due to the fact that you are going out in the evening more frequently, staying out later, and ending the night with a warm enthusiastic body, not necessarily in your own bed. Therefore, your start-up time on some mornings is longer than it was during your marital period. Plan your evenings with an eye toward the next day's schedule. If you have an early, busy next day, the female of the night before should be one you have known for a while and who does not require programming. Likewise, new females who require a detailed plot should be scheduled for an occasion when the following day is a holiday or fairly free.

Advanced planning of this nature will simplify screwing time and increase the pleasure of sex for both you and your friend.

Your male friends will also be particularly useful in another ticklish area. Now that you are single again, many of your married male friends will look to you to arrange surreptitious dates for them. If you have handled your stories convincingly, they believe that you have an endless supply of females ready to leap at your bidding. Unfortunately, this is not true, and should you be stupid enough to fix up a married man with one of your former female friends or, even stupider, with someone whom you're seeing occasionally but don't really care for, you may expect substantial abuse (and you clearly deserve it). However, there are unattached females who are not particularly scrupulous about the marital status of the men they go out with. With your inexperience you will hardly be in a position to judge which of the females you know have scruples that might prevent them from dating married men. But those male friends who have been at the bachelor business for a while should be able to handle the situation and accommodate this kind of request. Certainly, there is no particular reason why you should go out of your way to provide this kind of favor, unless of course you have a special reason. Arrangements with hookers and call girls for these unfortunate marrieds can be handled in the same fashion.

·11·

Her Mother Never Called
Her Incredible and
Her Mother Was Right

Sex in the latter days of your marriage, you must admit, was as dead as the marriage itself, and if not quite dead, certainly terminal. Hence, you are not unlike a survivor of a plane crash deposited in a vast desert. Because you are a survivor, you wander aimlessly through the heat and sand without water, when suddenly, without warning, before you glistens a pool of scum-covered, brackish, rank, uninviting water. You race toward it and hurl yourself blindly, hysterically, into it, consuming it in great gulps. The heat, of course, has destroyed your judgment so that you are convinced you are drinking sparkling Perrier. It is the same with the first "grand passion" of your rebach life. Your tastes are so warped, your mind so twisted, your recent sex life so nonexistent that you will feel as though you have met the world's most refreshing female.

The fact of the matter is that you have met a woman who recognized you for the sitting duck that you are. The female you bumped into understood the extent of your misery and moved in on you like a red soldier ant through the Brazilian jungle, sweeping through and conquering all in her path. You, dear rebach, were had. She said:

"You have great depth." (And you listened and forgot that so does an empty carton.)

"Your wife didn't know how lucky she was."

"How could she ever let you get away?"

"Your children sound fantastic. They will be in trouble without you around."

"You have unbelievable drive."

"You cannot help being successful."

"You are truly a man." (Whatever the hell that is supposed to mean.)

"You remind me of . . . Robert Redford, Jimmy Connors, Paul Newman, Burt Reynolds, Albert Einstein, Horatio Alger."

"You are beautifully sensitive and gentle."

"I don't know how you can possibly do all the things you do and do them so well."

Whatever else she could say to feed your ego, she said. Don't for a minute consider the things that you heard to be intelligent. They were inane and stupid, and clichéd, but they were said by a smart woman who knew that she must say inane and stupid things to you in your condition. The fact is, you believed them.

JERK!

And you will recall even more clearly the things that were said to you when you were in bed with her, and you will recall that you believed those things, too.

JERK!

Can you not also remember when your first really smart nickel-psychiatrist friend said to you, "Don't trap yourself with the first woman you meet"?

You justified your relationship with the age-old adage. "You don't understand. This is different." But you know now that it is never different, it's just that everyone thinks it is.

You responded in the classic manner—with a lot of nonsense:

"I've known a lot of women. They're just good lays, and when I want to move them out, I just pack their bags and do so. But this one is different."

"I get depressed, so I need her."

"I get lonely, so I need her."

"I've got to be more than just a lousy statistic, so I need her!"

"The whole goddamned world has tumbled down around my head, so I need her."

"I need this woman to get my head straight." (Unfortunately, when she fully straightens it you may wish it was crooked again.)

"She's a sweet, charming girl; she never asks for a thing."

"There is no way I can get hurt. I know how to take care of myself." The ultimate self-deception. You may take care of yourself so well that you end up temporarily trapped with her and looking for a way out.

Despair not. This first grand passion is a necessary part of rebaching. What you are really doing is getting used to having good sex again. Your infatuation may be translated as follows:

"I can really talk with her." (Translation: sex is unbelievable.)

"She really understands me." (Translation: sex is unbelievable.)

"We have such wonderful rapport." (Translation: sex is unbelievable.)

With wonderment, you will now recall the mess you created when you first brought her into your life, because at that time you were still married, although separated. Even though the amazing revitalization of the old gonads directed you to stay home alone with her as much as possible, you had to make a show of taking her out. In the beginning you chose restaurants carefully. The care you took in this regard had nothing to do with the food or the ambiance; rather, you wished to avoid running into old friends, possibly even older relatives. The undercover effort brought you both even closer. Finding restaurants off the normal trails blazed during your marriage provided excitement. Finally you found a place lacking both ambiance and decent food; but it did have absolute privacy because few people dined there. Because you were one of the rare customers, both of you became great friends with the bartender/owner or waiter/owner. The owner, never before having had a regular customer, was so pleased that he saw to it that the food, from time to time, was almost palatable. Soon the two of you had romanticized the dump into "our place."

Eventually you expanded your horizons, steeling yourselves to meet old acquaintances. You went to the movies and then the theater. Finally you got divorced and all wraps were off.

Somewhere in the middle of this relationship, but early on, while you were still unable to do anything about it, you and she started talking about how nice life would be if you didn't have the enormous pressures of a divorce, and how much fun it would be to be married. For a while you believed that indeed it might be fun. This pipe dream continued through the pre-divorce period.

Very quickly you found that the demands of your new female were such that you got the odd feeling that you somehow were married to two women (to her and to your estranged spouse). Though you didn't feel like a bigamist, it was not an entirely pleasant feeling. Occasionally you would meet male friends who had new female friends and begin to feel twinges of envy and regret that you were so totally locked in. Soon you were thinking that sex might be "unbelievable" with some other females.

Having made that discovery, the question becomes how to unstick yourself from this dumb relationship. By now it has indeed become a dumb relationship.

There is the direct approach, which you are not ready for. This is called honesty, and you say exactly what you feel—that you would like to end the relationship and take a look around at the world. But, unfortunately, at this point in your life it is highly unlikely that you have achieved the maturity or wisdom to do this. So, once again, your approach must be dishonest, and even in dishonesty you face problems. In the beginning it is easy to say any number of things that will get you free for one or two nights:

"I want to visit my parents, and they wouldn't understand our relationship."

"I have to work late at the office."

"I have regular corporation meetings on Tuesday nights, so we can't see each other."

Since you used these lies with your wife while you were committing adultery with her, she is not going to believe you unless she is a total dunce, which is unlikely. Nevertheless, she may begin to get the message that you want out. It is a somewhat harder step to suggest that you only get together on weekends. The beginning of the end is trumpeted by the line, "Why don't we each go out once in a while with someone else during the week."

When you have reached accord on going out during the week, you are probably now facing jealousy. Without question, *you* will be extremely jealous of her new male friends, even though this new routine was your idea.

With great pain and anguish, you will have on weekends any number of discussions about who she has been going out with and if she has gone to bed with him. Likewise, she will make similar inquiries. Because you are intellectually superior, you will lie and say you have not, and for some reason, probably because she is dealing honestly, she will believe you. And because she is dealing honestly, she will tell you the truth. The first time she tells you that she has slept with Joe/Pete/Frank, you will go totally ape. Though the average psychiatrist may tell you that you should not object to her sleeping with another man because she is receiving love, and though intellectually you may be able to accept the idea of her receiving love, it is impossible for you to accept this physical act.

In your state of enraged jealousy (much of which you will actually feel), you now have the perfect opportunity to end the damn relationship.

Take advantage of it.

If not ended abruptly and soon, you will suffer through a number of false starts and stops with the same woman, each of them more painful than the one before.

There are situations in which this entanglement is even more involved; for instance, if you gave your first grand passion a key to your apartment, and she moved in, or if your first grand passion is still living with her husband and is waiting for you to get a divorce.

If she has a key to your apartment, get a locksmith and change your lock. This should be done at the moment of your greatest anger, preferably without her knowledge. At the same time, pack her clothes and set the cases in the hall. Be sure, however, you are not present when she arrives at your apartment. It probably would be better to call her and tell her what you have done. Even though what you've done is a low stunt, the phone call will make you feel better.

As for problem number two, what this particular female requires (even more than possession of you) is a little honesty—probably available only through a psychiatrist. Her thinking that her future happiness is contingent upon your getting a divorce and then marrying her is a form of insanity. Your advice should be practical: "If you are truly unhappy, get out of your marriage and then let's talk about it."

As you escape from this first relationship, you must simply and continually keep in mind that a multiplicity of relationships is an avenue of growth.

You will ultimately reach your nirvana, but it will require your answering the question "Suppose I lose her?" with "Then all I have to do is spend the rest of my life enjoying my freedom."

Enormous emotional feelings will descend upon you as a result of the ending of this chapter of your life. It is one of the few times that writing is permitted, and whether it be poetry, song, or prose, you should feel free to write at length about your former Juliet. In view of the fact that your talents are something less than those of Shakespeare, Longfellow, Hoagy Carmichael or John Denver, it is probably wise to press your words, along with a wild rose, between the pages of your family Bible, and forget it. Under no circumstances mail your opus for the thought of this embarrassing document in the hands of others will haunt you for as long as you live. In your possession, it will become the beginning of your private joke book. Here is the work of some former rebaches:

> Please make up your mind.
> Which one will it be?
> You can't love another,
> And be here with me.

Or try this couplet, used but untested by time,

> Love had left me
> For another life.
> Still clouds of pain do not obscure
> Visions of my wife.

Or this,

> Where did it go?
> Did it really disappear?
> Was it me or she?
> Dare I hope it reappear?

It will, it surely will.

One problem remains. Suppose she has already left her husband without benefit of divorce, or even with it at your behest, and moved in with you and is waiting for you to get a divorce so she can marry you. That is a pip.

And so, with her timely departure, the doors have slammed shut (literally) on the first stage of your new life. Accompanied by the soft, muted tones of Gabriel's horn, the pearly gates now slowly swing open on the second act of your rebach life.

Your first grand passion will probably take one last shot at you, always in writing, either prose or poetry. Her missive will attempt sincerity, and if you are not forewarned of its power, it can be as tempting as the sirens in Homer's *Odyssey* and drown out the sweet, safe sound of Gabriel's horn.

Most likely, she will skip the poetry and make her last effort in simple prose.

You must keep in mind that no matter what you are reading, and no matter how delicately or charmingly she has written, she is simply saying: "You rotten bastard. I want you back."

The phrases will be something like the following:

"My very dear friend, you are a stubborn, blind man when you wish to be."

"I hope you know me well enough by this time to realize I have no axe to grind. Certainly this is not sour grapes. I only want to be your friend and confidante, and that was all I have ever wanted."

"When we parted, I said the things I said because I was operating with the eyes and ears of a woman on the defensive."

"I'm in a totally depressed state of mind, but I don't want you to worry."

"Don't be so hard on me for caring; it's my nature. I'm not pushing. Pushing is desperation and I'm not desperate."

"You gave me your best. I know that. I can ask for no more. It is important for us to continue as friends."

"If you think this is bullshit, and you tear up the letter, you tear up our friendship."

So let's be friends? No. Tear up the letter!

·12·

A Place to Lay My Head and a Few Other Things

Just as the old baby tooth falls from the mouth of a seven-year-old, leaving a bloody gap that slowly is filled with a brand-new permanent tooth, so does the most interesting stage of your bachelor life begin. As a matter of fact, just as the seven-year-old feels no more than an occasional twinge as the new tooth grows in, so will you hardly be aware (except also for an occasional twinge) of your passage into the second stage.

To begin with, there is your apartment. By this time, the four-walled escape pad you have been living in is no longer worthy of you. You now need a place not merely for eating and sleeping and love making, but a place in which to live.

The location should be as "in" as your budget will allow. By this time you should have found the action, and that is where you want to live. The building should have style, dignity, and in spite of this, be loaded with singles, preferably females. (If the town is right, follow the stewardesses.) Such a building is certainly more conducive to your new lifestyle than a building whose halls are loaded with tricycles and baby carriages.

You want a building of your peers, and peers have

nothing to do with age, but rather with advanced non-marital status. The apartment itself is no longer to be treated as a crash pad, but it should have sufficient space to accommodate you, your hobbies, occasional visits from children, and more frequent visits from females.

Furnishing this new home is an image-making effort best handled with professional assistance. The term professional assistance excludes helpful mothers, loving girlfriends, friends' wives or friendly architects. Helpful mothers will furnish to suit their image of you as their clean-cut American son, and by this time you should no longer be that person. Friendly girlfriends will furnish on the basis of how they would like to live if you should marry them. Friends' wives will offer to contribute their castoffs, but these will do little more than fill space and should be passed along to a grateful charity. Good-guy architects will be helpful in the beginning, but they will not have the time to follow through on any of the plans concocted on the backs of bar napkins when you were both half-bagged. This is not a do-it-yourself project. Talent and taste (not merely thinking you have great taste) mean a lot more than simply recognizing an attractive chair, fabric, or lamp in a *House Beautiful* ad.

There is simply no substitute for a good decorator. There are two kinds of decorators—homosexual and straight—and they come in two categories. There is the decorator who operates independently, charging retail prices for everything he purchases (wholesale). He will tell you that he can work within any budget that you establish.

He is as expensive as hell.

Then there is the decorator who is employed by a department store. He will walk through the store with you, buying the furniture from the store, and charge no fee to speak of. You will pay only the retail department store price, and he will work on a budget.

He is cheaper.

There are some advantages to the former. That guy will design original furniture for you. He will also pick out material, show you a one-inch swatch, explain that it will look marvelous on an eleven-foot couch, and you have no choice except to trust him because the swatch is so small. He will do floor plans, sketches, layouts, designs. He will drag you to furniture warehouses all over your community and outside of it. When he is all finished, he will have spent a lot of your money, but he will have fully equipped your apartment right down to the pencil on your night table. Of course, you will only have a limited idea in advance of what your place will look like.

He will also have collected enormous sums in advance. Because the expensive furniture that he has ordered is custom-made, you will probably have to move into a totally empty apartment, sleep in a sleeping bag and sit on milk crates because the delivery dates of the furniture have not been met. He will also, when the furniture arrives, flutter around the apartment, not liking some of it because it wasn't made exactly right, and attempt to send it back to have it corrected. You will, because you are intelligent, tell him it's O.K. the way it is; otherwise, your lease will be half over before you have any furniture at all. He will also hang your pictures, arrange your ashtrays, and probably get a photographer to take a picture of the place as it looks the day before you move in. Save the picture, for it will never look the same, or as good, again.

In the case of the second decorator, he will also prepare sketches, but they will be limited, nothing more than layouts of where your furniture will fit. However, in addition to the lesser expense, there is also the tremendous advantage of seeing the eleven-foot couch fully covered so that you will not be shocked when the one-inch square of material turns into thirty yards of upholstery. In addition, department stores tend to be more realistic about furniture delivery dates, and delivery is generally made when indicated. The major disadvantage here is that your apartment can, if not artfully done, look like the furniture sales floor of the major department store in your town.

Just on general principle, don't buy suites of things. Avoid deals where you purchase at a fixed price matching bed, chest, end tables, lamps, lampshades, etc. They generally look tacky.

Both decorators will deliver certain speeches, and that's all they are—just speeches. For when someone says, ''I must know your personality and then get it into the apartment,'' or ''The apartment must be you,'' or

"The apartment must reflect your sensitivity, strength, intelligence, humor, intuitiveness, and charm," it is fun to listen, but it's bullshit. For if you were to ask yourself what color humor is, or what shape table will reflect intelligence, or what lampshade is most indicative of strength, you will find yourself in the world of the absurd. Nevertheless, it is part of their *modus operandi*, so enjoy it.

In spite of the fact that the pronoun "he" has been used in connection with decorators, you are far better off with a female decorator. She will probably have her own ideas about what a playboy bachelor's apartment should look like and will carry these ideas out without allowing you to mess them up with your own taste. The result can be extraordinary. Unfortunately, the average male decorator has either been warped by his own ego, ruined by his own divorce, or is homosexual and his taste, although certainly good, will not include the ambiance that appeals to female fantasies. Avoid colors like sunset red, or turtleback green, or moonlight yellow, and insist on simplicity. The goddamn thing is either red or green or yellow. Leave the cute and the coy to someone else's definition.

The bedroom should have a red carpet. It should also have red drapes that match the red bedspread, and the ceiling should be painted a red that matches as closely as possible all the other reds in the room. The room should be sparsely furnished. It should contain one extraordinarily large bed. There should be a table on either side of the bed, with one drawer. The drawer is critical (explanation to follow). There should be one inconspicuous reading lamp on one side of the bed only, yours. (Simultaneous reading should take place in the public library.)

All other light sources should be indirect and focused on the ceiling to create a glowing crimson. Don't for a minute believe that red is a hard color; when the indirect lights are on, they will achieve a soft explosion of pink. There also should be a telephone jack in the room so that you can have a phone at your bedside when you are alone. Under no circumstances should you have a permanently connected bedroom phone that might ring when you are otherwise occupied. Incidentally, make sure that any phone in the apartment has a cut-off switch so that it will not ring when you would least like it to ring.

The bedroom can be approached in two ways when you enter it for the first time with a new female. Which way you choose depends to a great extent upon your style.

It can be casually serious: "This is a decorator-designed room, and I think it is a little bit heavy, but my decorator insisted that it be a comfortable room in which to rest and relax."

Or it can be treated casually with Boy Scout humor: "I told my decorator I wanted a great seduction room. Did you ever see anything like this?" At which point you chortle.

Depending upon your delivery, either approach could work, and the soft fusion of redness will knock her on her ass, which is where you want her anyhow.

. A PLACE TO LAY MY HEAD .

The other critical room in the apartment is the entrance way. The lighting and colors in this area are totally unimportant. What is important is that this area contain the largest bar you can afford, a bar that can substitute at all times for intimate dining.

The most unimportant piece of furniture you can buy is a dining room table. It is highly unlikely that you will, at this stage of your life, give dinner parties, but if you feel lost without some sort of dining facility, buy something that folds up into something else and can be used as something else, and which, if necessary, can seat people for dining.

Also essential in the apartment are candles in metal containers that can be safely allowed to burn when you are not around, and the best hi-fi stereo that you can afford with speakers that function in the bedroom as well as other areas. Try to arrange to have a shut-off switch next to your bed.

Candles create a romantic effect if allowed to burn safely with you not around. When you leave for a date that has some probability of your bringing her back, there is nothing quite as dramatic or that announces as loudly what your apartment is all about than opening the door to the dark with appropriate candles casting flickering shadows about the room.

If the red bedroom doesn't attract the moth to the flame and the candles are smoky, consider the following:

Dimmer switches in critical spots—particularly effective if the candles burn down while you are out of the apartment.

Second only in importance to your bed is a heavy, thick, plush, long-haired carpet on the living room floor. Round and white if you can afford it, and unobstructed by furniture. It is often easier to drop casually on the carpet, bringing her down with you, than to take her into the bedroom, unless there is total willingness on her part.

If your apartment is small, a platform bed substituting for a couch can be convenient as occasionally romance begins while you are still drinking.

And there are water beds.

There are other accouterments absolutely required in the proper presentation of your apartment. A Museum of Modern Art calendar, paintings by an unknown painter (because they are cheap), a hude sculpture, hanging and standing plants (real ones, not artificial, even though you may become frustrated trying to keep them alive), and a harness brass collection, or, if you don't happen to like harness brass, an antique collection of pulleys. All of this you can talk about, and none of this will have cost you a hell of a lot.

Now for the contents of that drawer in the bedside table mentioned earlier. It should hold an electric vibrator, with proper working lifetime batteries; Lubriderm lotion; and prophylactics (to be used only if she is not on the pill and doesn't have an IUD—you don't want to fool around with an abortion). And, of course, a Gideon Bible.

. A PLACE TO LAY MY HEAD .

The shelves in the bathroom-bedroom area should contain brushes and combs in sufficient quantities that your brunette friend doesn't find a brush with blonde hair, and vice versa. You should also have guest toothbrushes, shower caps, and an ample supply of Vitabath, which sweetens the bathwater, generates ample bubbles, is fun to bathe in (particularly when you are not alone), and leaves no ring.

The bar should be stocked with certain esoteric beverages (aquavit, tequila, sake), an ample supply of wine in a wine rack, and, whether you use it or not, a cigarette box filled with cigarette papers and marijuana (you can tell a fascinating, original story about how you acquired it), and a little machine to roll cigarettes for you.

As for the dreary but necessary business of brooms, dishes, pots, pans, cleansers, rags, mops, sponges and "pink pads," let's hope that one of your current female friends can be prompted into taking a trip to the supermarket to buy you these things. Basic foodstuffs, such as catsup, mustard, mayonnaise, salt and pepper, can be provided in the same way. More important, however, is the slowly learned ability to cook for survival as well as for seduction. Cooking for survival should be as infrequent as possible; you can take vitamin supplements and make trips to restaurants. Cooking for seduction is of far greater complexity, but, when properly understood, the simplest thing in the world.

Inviting a female friend to your apartment for a home-cooked Italian dinner requires some imagination but little cooking. On the bar or table place candles, silverware, and dishes (arranged, if you know how, stacked if you can't be bothered); a large loaf of Italian bread and a very large knife for dramatic effect; an opened can of anchovies plus some pimentos arranged on one plate in whatever way they fell out of the can; and spaghetti. The spaghetti is served last.

Spaghetti for two is cooked by simply opening up a package of Ronzoni, taking out half the package, breaking that half in half, dropping it into a pot of boiling water, and allowing it to boil for as long as it says to boil on the package. Sprinkle in some salt. When the spaghetti is cooked, dump it into a strainer and run cold water over it. This, in theory, washes off the starch; in practice it makes the spaghetti slightly cold. However, do not despair, for in another pot you dump a jar of supermarket spaghetti sauce in which you sprinkle a little pepper. The only reason you sprinkle in the pepper is so you are able to say that this is prepared with your own special recipe. When you dump the hot sauce on the lukewarm spaghetti, you once again have hot spaghetti with hot sauce, which you put into a bowl and serve. As the *pièce de résistance*, you serve espresso coffee. This means you need two little cups and two little saucers, two tiny spoons, and a jar of instant espresso. It is made exactly like instant coffee. To show that you know what you are about, you drop in two pieces of lemon peel. Finally, in the middle of the table or bar next to the candles, you place at least one bottle of Italian red wine, with a second in reserve.

If you have earlier suggested that she come over for

cocktails, and there is just the two of you, the simplest approach is caviar. Don't worry about whether she likes it or not. It won't matter because you will serve it with ample cocktails. Caviar comes in two basic brands: red (cheap), black (expensive). In either case, open the jar, put it in the center of a plate, and surround it with half of a package of Philadelphia cream cheese on one side and chopped onions on the other. If you want to be truly stylish, add some parsley, and if you want to go overboard, boil an egg and chop that up. Finish up the whole thing with a separate plate of assorted crackers. You have now created a professional cocktail party. Double-check that the liquor is plentiful.

There is, of course, the ultimate cop-out, but cleverly handled, it can be tremendously effective. "Come on over and we'll order something in."

This requires no knowledge of cooking, but rather of who delivers what from where.

There is no town so small or so dead that it does not have its own Chinese restaurant with delivery service or its own Italisn *ristorante* with pizza to go. To make this kind of ordering interesting and essentially romantic, you should master a few simple Chinese phrases and Italian one-liners.

Operating from memory (or, better still, from a prepared list carefully concealed so that it appears that you are operating from memory), you should be able to suggest some exotic-sounding food. This is not the time to try two from column A and one from Column B. It is the time for pressed duck—Cantonese, or *moo shu* pork—Mandarin, or hot and spicy shrimp—Szechuan.

Clearly, it is not the time, even if you like them, for spareribs, chicken chow mein, chop suey, or fortune cookies. Even if your salivary glands long for spareribs, this food is greasy as hell, and you will find it off-putting and sticky to reach over and kiss a greasy woman.

As for the Italian, once again use a hidden list. Avoid spaghetti, spaghetti with meat balls, spaghetti with red sauce, spaghetti with clam sauce, and ravioli. Substitute veal *saltimbocca*, or steak *pizziola* with peppers, or shrimp *fra diavolo*.

Unless you and this particular female dig the stuff, and even then it is questionable practice, you should never order, or bring home, food from McDonald's, Kentucky Fried Chicken, or Arthur Treacher's Fish and Chips; nor should you order salami and cheese sandwiches with pickles from the local delicatessen. (These items are only permissable after sex—if consumed before, there may never be an after.)

As a final comment on food in your apartment, always keep crackers and cheese available for late evening snacks to go with a cup of coffee or "one for the road." The harder the cheese, the longer it will last, so purchase a round of cheese and an unusual assortment of crackers.

Peanut butter and jelly are out.

As a result of *your* culinary efforts, there should be some invitations to females' houses for dinners which they will cook. If you are able to eat cold spaghetti, there is very little that she can come up with that you will not enjoy tremendously. But if by chance the gastronomic delight you had hoped for turns out instead to give you gastric indigestion, plead that you're on a diet. If you're lucky, a begging dog will be conveniently present.

No matter what, arrive with a bottle of wine (or two, if you think a second will be required). You can also send or bring flowers, but keep in mind that liquor is quicker. One school of thought maintains that a gift of flowers on Valentine's Day, or when you are coming over for dinner, is a lot of bullshit. Flowers for no reason at all is a far greater promotional ploy.

·13·

Facelift Your Ego

Let vanity be your guide. It's time to adopt a style of dress which suits your new single personality, even if that personality is totally different from your business personality. Begin to let your clothes do some of the talking for you, whether they be faded dungarees and cowboy boots or silk suits and patent leather shoes. Allow a style to develop. It will if you want it to, and don't spent a lot of time resisting clothing temptations that might have been ridiculed, criticized, or otherwise put down during your marriage.

Also remember there are no truly great fat bachelors. Likewise, there are no truly great fat rebaches. If you are fat, or think you are fat, or if too many of the females you go with comment about your weight, do something about it. There are three hundred and thirty-two diets you can go on and all of them work. It is merely a question of hewing to a diet religiously for about six weeks. Regrettably, your biggest problem will not be the temptation of ice cream, candy, and whipped cream cake, but liquor. Somehow, for six weeks, even if you don't put yourself totally on the wagon, you should cut down on the booze. If you are still convinced you need three scotches to relax, try one and a half. You might also keep in mind that you burn up calories when you have sex; fucking is not only fun but healthy. Even doctors agree.

If you really get carried away with the new you and want to sound super macho, there are lines like:

"I do 100 push-ups a day."

"I have a 28-inch waist and 42-inch shoulders." (No one carries a measuring tape around.)

"I finished the marathon in under three hours."

"I jump rope 40 minutes daily."

"My latest stress test indicates that . . ."

"My cardiovascular system is incredibly improved."

Some of it may become reality if you say it often enough.

Whether it has to do with new clothes or crash diets or a flashy lifestyle, your ego in its new state of freedom will be vain about many things, particularly about your sexual powers.

Sexual vanity takes many forms. It may be expressed in terms of the number of orgasms you can accomplish in an evening, or in terms of the number of orgasms you are capable of helping your female to achieve. In both cases, your success is probably due more to the female involved than to your abilities. But your pride is in direct proportion to the number of times you or she will come. The greater the number of orgasms, the greater your pride in your ability as a sexual athlete.

Sexual acrobatics can boost your ego. The female's

gyrations and moans of ecstasy will give you pleasure. Because your sexual ego so badly needs to recover from your marriage experience, you should be able to convince yourself that there is a direct relationship between the female's body-language of love making and your abilities as a lover. You are more than likely overestimating her abilities. But this is understandable, for on the rare occasions when you and the Bitch made love, your love making was soundless and motionless. It no doubt became nothing more than a "let's get it over with already" affair. Your former wife probably "submitted" to, or appeared to put up with, your entreaties merely because you pestered her. Now noise and motion are exciting, and you feel like you are at the center of an earthquake registering six on the Richter scale.

Unless you doubt the sincerity of the female, the single greatest compliment you can receive is for her to say to you, when it's all over, "You're a great fuck." When this happens, if it happens (and if it is believable), your vanity will have reached its maximum level.

But if you allow your vanity to get too big (no pun intended), the result can be self-destructive:

Impotence.

If your love making has been indiscriminate enough, you will, from time to time, "come a cropper." Vanity will lead you down this road. Once having convinced yourself that you are a super lover, convincing yourself that there are no circumstances under which you cannot perform is easy. Your sex life prior to rebaching was limited because you were often unable to perform due to boredom, hatred, and aggravation. Your inconsistent performance at home was derided by your wife, an expert in derision. The castration complex induced by the trauma of a bad marriage is a neurosis that you must overcome. You must reverse the course of personal history. Having rediscovered your love-making ability, you must be all the more aware of the psychological dangers of temporary impotence; because of your past history, temporary failure can be dreadful unless understood. The fact is that there are a number of circumstances in which this disaster can, and will, strike. The danger of this temporary blow is that you may think you have been stricken with a chronic illness. This can intimidate you and make you afraid of exposing yourself in the future, both emotionally and physically. You may become preoccupied with the problem. You may dwell on it, have a second episode, dwell on it some more, have a third and then a fourth, and spend some thousands of dollars in psychotherapy trying to get back to the beginning. Ego and vanity notwithstanding, your body will absorb punishment only up to a point. You must learn to ignore the mind which will say, "How can I fail when she's got such a great face, ass, legs, tits?" because you can.

Recognize the danger symptoms. Learn the exact relationship between flaccidity, or semi-flaccidity, and the amount of liquor that you may have consumed. Understand the relationship between the amount of sleep that you may or may not have gotten and your ability to function.

Don't ever overestimate your energy level or under-estimate the effects of liquor or lack of sleep. Most important, when you are temporarily impotent, don't ever overestimate the ability of a woman to change that state merely because she has talented hands, legs, or mouth. This is an ego-trip that women often take without prompting, for all women love to believe that their charms and abilities cannot be withstood by a mortal male. The truth of the matter is that her charms will only drive you back into the protective shell you used when you were married. When you are feeling like the living dead, even a Venus de Milo with arms will not awaken you.

Recognize when to be affectionate, but not sexual.

A final word of advice. If in spite of your best efforts you have been turned down or off, treat it in the most impersonal manner; accept the fact that, if you try enough times, you are going to face some turn-downs. No man, woman, or goldfish can be everything to everybody.

It is hardest to accept a turn-down when you have finally gotten a woman across the threshold of your apartment. But this too will occur—and not merely because your decorator did a lousy job. Just because she accepted your invitation to have a nightcap or to hear the new Bette Midler record, do not automatically suppose that you are about to make the great romantic scene. To protect yourself in this kind of situation, assume, when she walks across the threshold, that you can assume nothing and must begin your romantic efforts afresh.

.FACELIFT YOUR EGO.

Certainly you can take a woman anyplace, including your apartment, and enjoy her as a friend. But unfortunately, the true male-female relationship carries with it sexual overtones (or undertones), and even though you may not head toward bed in the beginning, bed will hang over your head like the great Sword of Damocles.

For the new you, agelessness is a goal to be striven for. When you find yourself attracted to a female who happens to be ten, fifteen, twenty, or twenty-five years younger, you should not talk about age. You should assume that she finds you, in spite of the age difference (which may or may not be apparent), more mature, more sophisticated, more intellectual, and more scintillating than younger guys she knows. If you cannot talk yourself out of your insecurity, then you may have to lie. The lie need not be so exaggerated as to make you young. If you're fifty (unless you happen to look sixty), you should easily be able to tell her that you're forty-two or forty-four. The lie will reduce the age difference, at least in your mind.

The fact is that most of the females to whom you will be attracted will be considerably younger. That is not the problem. The problem is the age of the men who generally surround younger females. Those men will appear to you to be much younger than you, and they probably will be. But, as much as you can, ignore the problem and assume that she does not regret your age. The average divorced male *has* to be older than the average male who has never been married.

When there is an age disadvantage, a lie will give you

strength, your maturity and sophistication will give you courage, and the money you spend on her will bring you success. It is equally true that the average rebach is quicker to buy flowers and presents and to spend than the average bachelor, who is still getting by on his looks and muscles. The average female with a brain in her head should instinctively prefer the former over the latter.

Eventually you will stop dwelling on the problem of your age. You can achieve your ends even if the competition looks like a working lifeguard and the object of your affection is a gum-chewing teenybopper.

Incidentally, once you do restructure your age, remember also to scale the age of your children and the length of time you were married. You can also say that you married very young. Obviously, if you have mentioned casually that you were married at twenty-five, you cannot shave your age to thirty-five unless you remember to make your fourteen-year-old son nine.

A woman's age should be of only passing importance if there are good vibrations.

Once you've begun to lie about your age, you must be consistent about it with everyone you know. You will confuse your friends and relatives. Ultimately, they will become so confused that they won't give a damn. By that time, you probably won't either.

It is almost totally destructive to have a girlfriend younger than your oldest son or daughter. You will think, "My God, when I was thirty she was only six years old" or "She wasn't even born when I had my first kid.'' She may say, ''President Kennedy's assassination made no impression on me because I was too young to remember it.'' She may also say, ''Just think, I was only three months old when you were wounded in the War.''

If these comments bother you, there is the classic response, ''If what you are trying to say is that I was busy fucking before you knew what the word meant, then you are correct.'' Age rarely matters to a woman unless she is interested in a serious relationship. In that event, you might want to restore a decade or two to yours if you are seriously interested in her. But acknowledging your age has got to mean that you are very serious, so why bother? Do you really want to be *that* serious?

·14·

It's Not Masters and Johnson But It's Functional

The rules and techniques of seduction that you'll now be following are a far cry from those you may recall from the prehistoric days prior to your marriage. Depending on your age, those days were either late pre-pill or early post-pill.

As a pre-pill bachelor, the drive to get laid, and certainly your success, were seriously hampered by the female's fear of pregnancy and its complications. You often felt like you were living in a pressure cooker. There were the times when her period should have occurred, but did not; then it became overdue, alarmingly so, then finally it appeared—or you had a problem.

In your effort to eliminate her fear of pregnancy, it was always possible to convince her that your interest in her was simply platonic; that you merely wanted a good, friendly companion. If you were successful, you romanced ("good friended") your way into bed. But you may also have been forced into a marriage because you later didn't have the nerve or know-how to be honest. That could in fact be how you got into your most recent ex-marriage.

. IT'S NOT MASTERS AND JOHNSON .

In those days, the joy of spontaneous love making was seriously hampered by the use of clammy, cold, sticky, wet prophylactics. Equally unappetizing was the examination at the end of the act to be certain that the balloon had not burst. Nor was spontaneity enhanced if, in the midst of your most dramatic passionate moments, you had to turn to your woman and ask, "Are you wearing a diaphragm?" If the answer to the question was negative, your bold courageous statement (she had to have the courage): "Under the circumstances we will practice coitus interruptus."

In most instances, making-out was a battle to overcome resistance, but then, unlike now, a much heartier battle.

The vocabulary of the pre-pill days was quaint, a language in and of itself. It included such terms as "scoring," "finger fucking," and, the ultimate statement, "going all the way." An archaic scenario, at best.

The script in the initial phase of the post-pillers was considerably easier: "What the hell!" It was liberation for the females, and they went to town. Many females who didn't become liberated later felt they missed the boat. That, however, was early in the post-pill era.

You are entering upon a latter day, a highly sophisticated sexual scene. In its own way, it is as highly structured as the earlier periods, except that resistance has dissipated into total freedom, which in reality has become absolute license. Nowadays your approach must be that of a mature adult seducer. This is an approach that you have had no opportunity to learn, an approach that long-time bachelors understand because they have grown with it. Your growth was stopped when you married. There is a lot of relearning to be done. The women you meet now will be light-years ahead of you because of the freedom they have lived with. If you were formerly an adulterer, the attitudes you held then (because you were still a husband and a full-time father) will be preposterous in your new society of freedom.

Along with this freedom, you will have to contend with the females' search for ''value'' in your ''relationship.'' They will look for common interests, and if you get too far into this, you can become as trapped as if you were married. Much to the woman's despair, at every turn you must deride, despise, and fail to understand the word ''relationship.''

In spite of what you hear during ''scotch talk'' at cocktail parties, a woman's first reaction to a man will be based on his physical appearance.

The woman who says that she is really more attracted to a man's mind than to his body is, at the very least, a liar. If she sees three men in a room, she will definitely want the best-looking of the group to approach her, or she, in her turn, will sashay up to this man.

If you are good-looking, you're halfway home, unless you foul up en route. But whether you are good-looking, ugly, or just ordinary, keep yourself reasonably well-groomed.

.IT'S NOT MASTERS AND JOHNSON.

Don't be a slob, for you will only attract the female counterpart, which is another slob.

Whether you meet at a political rally, at a cocktail party, in a museum, or walking the dog, you should appear to be gentle and sensitive, but at the same time aggressive, exhibiting as much macho as possible.

Be humble, but with an emormous positive ego.

Be earthy and intellectual.

You also must be polite.

You should like children and dogs, admire cats, enjoy gardening and flower arranging, and at the same time talk about your tennis and golf games and how high you jumped the last time you went horseback riding.

You must create an image, even if it's a ridiculous one, and you must learn to be able to project it on the spot, leaving a vague impression that you are indeed all of these things. You must also spend considerable time listening.

There is an art to listening and appearing interested even while being bored out of your skull. With practice, you will learn to nod at the right time, smile when it appears to be appropriate, and avoid a glassy-eyed look. You must learn to recognize a look of attention in others so that you can determine whether your words are creating the right image.

If you are a top quality listener, you will hear, from time to time, "You're a great person to talk to." Translation: you kept your mouth shut, didn't interrupt, and appeared to be interested.

If, while you're talking, your mind wanders to another female in the room, don't look at her. If the conversation is dull, look at your watch; the message is obvious and brutal, but effective.

Should a female compliment you on being a good listener, make a subtly humble, memorable reply: "I've learned that you can learn very little when you are talking."

Don't be concerned that you may nauseate her with your saccharine sweetness. More than likely, the effect will be to create the impression that you are extraordinarily sensitive.

Because most females enjoy talking about themselves, a brilliant opening gambit is usually "Why don't you tell me about yourself." If this does not bring the desired result, and you get "There is nothing to tell," assume either that she is a dud or, more interestingly, that she would rather have you ask, "What can I tell you about me?" If she replies, "Nothing," then give up the ghost entirely. If she says, "Anything," begin almost anyplace, except by discussing schools that you both might have attended or friends whom you both might know. Skip the phrase, "Where did you go to school?" It is terribly unoriginal and does not do anything for your image. Also, there is the possibility that she didn't go to school.

Better opening lines, carefully considered like the opening lines in a play, would be "What do you read?" (you are literate and are acknowledging that she is as well) or "Are you interested in . . . ?" (opera, music, art).

However, whichever area you choose in the arts, you must be informed, at least on the surface, about the fad of the moment. If you think that faddists are into opera, remember the names of one or two popular opera stars and read a criticism of an opera somewhere. *Madame Butterfly* is reasonably well-known, Puccini is an easy name to pronounce, and the libretto is as simple as Mother Goose.

There are, of course, other areas, again depending upon the moment. "Do you jog?" "Do you play touch football?"

In the case of jogging, if she says no, you can describe in detail and in length the benefits of jogging and create the impression that you are either a super-jock or a super health nut. If she confides that she does play touch football, it is time to seek greener pastures. Should she respond with something like "No, I don't, but I'd love to," don't take her up on it: this is not the way to spend a Sunday afternoon. Female touch football players are either so uncoordinated that the simplest athletic endeavor will break a finger, bust a tooth, or strain a muscle, or so ferocious that you will think you are facing an incarnate Red Grange. Because you are a true gentleman, you will try to avoid hurting her and in the process get clobbered. This kind of endeavor can never prove valuable.

Astrology is, of course, something that everyone

talks about from time to time, and most people know little more than their astrological sign.

You open with: "What sign were you born under?"

Regardless of their sign, you must immediately respond enthusiastically with: "My God, I'm a ————! (Taurus, Leo, Libra, Virgo, etc.) Do you realize that our signs work perfectly together?"

Or memorize one line of total gibberish and make it sound monumental: "Virgo is in the ascendancy and your moon and sun are in Aquarius and have stabilized."

Be certain her only knowledge of astrology is what she reads in a local newspaper column. But you must know all of the astrological signs. If you are not sure of the date the signs begin and end, don't get too deeply involved in the subject.

Similarly, palm reading is an excellent conversational ploy. It requires a knowledge of only three lines in your palm: the heart-line, the life-line, and a series of lines which, when properly connected, create an "M" referred to as the money line. It helps a lot if the "M" exists in your palm because you can say that it indicates that you will always have money.

Other simple nuances are good to know. If a hand is extended toward you when you start reading the palm in a cupped fashion, you can assume this to mean that she is extremely open and generous. If she extends her palm flat, ignore it. A flat palm means she's uptight and hardnosed. When you read her palm, always note a long life-line and always comment that she has had a serious illness or accident. Every female at one time or another has exaggerated a migraine into a brain tumor, a head cold into double pneumonia, and a stomach ache into appendicitis.

The clinching line in palm reading, after the proper time spent staring at the palm, is:

"There is no question about it. Someone very near to you is jealous of what you do, or are, or know."

There isn't a woman walking who won't believe one of those.

Palm reading, you will find, carries with it another great advantage. It creates, for the first time, one of the most important elements in a male-female relationship. Touching!

Under no circumstances should you make yourself too much of an expert in any one area. For too great expertise may eliminate the flexibility you need if someone does not happen to be interested in tennis, football, astrology, palm reading, opera, or whatever.

Be peripherally informed about many subjects, uninformed in depth on any.

As often as possible, you should try to establish yourself as an intellectual. Not necessarily a super intellectual, but certainly a reasonably average intellectual. Remember how often you have heard:

"When I first met him, he wasn't that good looking, but when you talk to him he sort of grows on you" (like a fungus). You must cash in on this.

There is no better method for appearing intellectual than being able to quote things. Proper quotes slipped into conversation with subtlety can crack the frigidity of the most ice-sculptured female.

How can honor not clearly appear as one of your great virtues when you solemnly quote Grantland Rice:

> When the one great scorer comes to write against your name,
> He marks not that you won or lost, but how you played the game.

All women like to believe that the men they are involved with, if nothing else, have at least a degree of sensitivity. Be grateful to Edna St. Vincent Millay for:

> My candle burns at both ends;
> It will not last the night;
> But ah, my foes, and oh, my friends—
> It gives a lovely light.

(The fact that a woman wrote these lines gives your character another dimension as well.)

Now that you have established your honor and sensitivity, your macho must also appear, and old Grantland Rice has done it again:

> Keep coming back with all you've got, without an alibi,
> If Competition trips you up or lands upon your eye,
> Until at last above the din you hear this sentence spilled:
> "We might as well let this bird through before we all get killed."

. IT'S NOT MASTERS AND JOHNSON .

To establish perserverance, grim determination, and singleness of purpose, a little masculine prose can be useful. Find a novel with a story that can be abbreviated and a punch line that is a pistol.

Mickey Spillane is a good author with whom to make your point. In a novel entitled *I, the Jury*, a hard-nosed detective finds his best friend murdered, proceeds through overwhelming odds to track down the murderer while falling passionately in love with a gorgeous woman, whom in the last chapter he discovers to be the killer. As she undresses and walks toward him naked, her hands reaching out, he shoots her in the stomach. The book ends:

> "How c-could you?" she gasped.
> I only had a moment before talking to a corpse, but I got it in.
> "It was easy," I said.

Dynamite. Magnificent, pure macho.

These are just suggestions and are not intended to be used by all. You must find your own style, illustrations, and quotations. It is the personality that makes the quotation effective. Just as quotations should be personally styled, it is equally appropriate to search for and, if necessary, create interesting phrases.

To indicate simplicity of accomplishment: "It's a hanger." "Easy comfort." "A piece of cake."

The simple phrase, "six of one and a half dozen of the other," becomes "six or two threes."

Boredom: "Game's not worth the candle."
Sprinkling your conversation with certain simplistic French or Italian phrases is useful.
Endearment: *"Ma cheri."* Or super endearment, requiring super memory: *"Mia cara, ti voglio tanto bene, tu sei tutta la mia vita."* (My love, I love you very much, you are my whole life.)
Cheap: *"Déclassé."*
However, your footwork with respect to these phrases must be individualized, for what cannot be done is to learn these by "the numbers" or by "the book."
It is time also to reassert your ego, an ego that, if not totally destroyed, has at least taken an incredible beating. This reassertion cannot be done without appropriate forethought and to no little extent without sufficient female compliments which will have come your way. (Psychiatric assistance helps also.) In place of the earlier reflexive attitudes, you will learn how to properly and definitively use the same "I":
"I can . . ."
"I will . . ."
"I do . . ."
"I want . . ."
"I know . . ."
"I think . . ."
"I need . . ."
There is a time for humility, there is a time for free spirit, a time for free thinking, and the great "I" will bring it out.
Ultimately, your expressions will be clear not only to

all the females around you, and they will love you for it, but also to yourself, and you'll love you for it.

Be good to yourself without limitation.

Though your relearned conversational techniques have been sufficiently developed to create a preliminary intellectual comradeship, the problem of refreshing your recollection with respect to the technique of bringing this comradeship into the realm of sexual contact (in the shortest possible time) is upon you.

The threshold to be crossed to accomplish reasonable sexual contact on some mature level begins with touching. Your prior experience in the subtleties of touching have either been forgotten or, for one reason or another, never used. So, you must consider yourself as embarking on a brand-new learning experience. Touching is literally a seventh sense. By the time your marriage had ended, that sense had gone the way of other marital comforts; you were much more into pure fucking and simple sensitive touching was an unknown.

The physical touching that you must learn is a creative process. It will reduce to rubble most sexual barriers, or it will quickly indicate to you that certain sexual barriers are insurmountable.

You can begin with simple casual conversation. When you are expressing a point of great significance (or of insignificance), it would be the norm to casually reach toward the female and emphasize the point by a light tap on her hand. If the hand should retreat, you may have discovered through her body language an insurmountable barrier. If there is no retreat, it should not be too difficult to tap again, and then again, and then finally to allow your hand to rest on hers. Quite obviously, you have soon reached the stage of holding hands, at which point the initial physical contact is made.

In any event, if you are physically touching her, you're headed in the right direction. It is certainly possible just to reach out and blatantly take her hand, but this is clumsy, can leave you feeling clumsy, and can turn an otherwise casual move into a monumental mistake. Subtlety at all times is a most effective technique.

Casual touching can include a "hail fellow well met" camaraderie. An arm flung softly across her shoulder will result either in her moving imperceptibly toward you or in an unbending, motionless reaction (in which event get your arm off). Whatever the result, it will be easily recognizable.

Other techniques: Brush poetically an imaginary speck of dust or dirt from her cheek. Touch her hair with a comment on how soft it is. The contact achieved by these techniques is without the risk of rejection.

There are some total negatives. Grabbing is never permissible, except the dramatic, momentary gesture of taking her strongly by her shoulders, pulling her toward you and saying anything at all, so long as it appears romantic (if she is prepared to accept the romantic challenge, the phrase can be totally inane or innocuous and it will work like great poetry).

There must at no time be urgency in the touching. The urgency, or apparent urgency, must be saved for moments further down the road when the advantages are obvious. The initial physical contact must be on the basis of: "Oh, what the hell, I've been there before—it would be nice, but it just isn't all that important."

If a woman starts to touch you, ignore everything that has gone before and immediately proceed forward with absolute confidence and haste. Don't expect this to happen too often. You can also use certain interesting phrases at a time like that which may work wonders. They are nothing other than direct, and sometimes for that reason they are all-powerful.

"Let's make love."

·15·

Miscellaneous Women and Their Miscellaneous Similarities

If there were a blood bank for good women, the need to type them would be unnecessary. But on the road from the place you are coming from to where you hope you are headed (in order to avoid passing yourself in both directions), it is essential that you understand the broad, general descriptions of females. It has been years since you had sufficient exposure to females to remember, and now is the time to remember what you have sadly forgotten.

Women may be classified, compartmentalized, characterized, and defined in detail. They do not in any instance reach a level of describable individuality. When they define themselves, the definitions are simplistic.

Once you have become a learned scholar, your sexual life with females, and even your nonsexual life with females, is no more difficult for you than the handling of kindergarten building blocks. If you express this in any way to any woman, you will be angrily challenged, but challenge notwithstanding, she will never totally recognize the gross nature of this insult, though it is deserved. (Women are predictable because they are followers with few leaders—in fashion, in child-rearing, and in love making.)

As to the specifics: there are females who equate sex and love, and this equation is mindlessly interchangeable by them. The women in this group feel they must fall in love in order to permit a sexual relationship. Love, a self-imposed trance for these women, is undefined. If the sex act occurs prior to the introduction of the love trance, then, in justification, a woman of this sort will predictably convince herself that sexual intercourse would never have occurred but for the fact that she was in love, an even more blatant self-induced mesmerization. It is interesting that with this woman, after fornication, you will not see or hear from her for days or weeks or months or ever. Your efforts to reach her will be unsuccessful, and if a phone call should connect, your entreaties will be unavailing. She cannot face the product of her trance or mesmerization; for that product is guilt.

Should, at some point in time, she become available to you again, you will discover that continuing the physical aspect of the relationship will require your reconfirming the trance (love). Then you must decide if reconfirmation is worth it. With such reconfirmation, you will have a woman who will respond to you in leech fashion and who will whiningly tyrannize, especially when ultimately she learns that your purpose was simply to get her into bed. She will feel that you have achieved new depths as a louse. So what!

There are other women who deal in language clichés, and even your rebach inexperience should be able to overcome these not too difficult single line statements. To be forewarned is to be forearmed:

"I'm old fashioned."

"We hardly know each other."

"Sex is a personal thing, and without a relationship (ugh!) it is nothing."

"What kind of girl do you think I am?" (The years that have passed during your marriage have not dissipated the basic stupidity of this phrase.)

"What will people say?"

All this female is attempting with these sad clichés is to say to you and to herself that sex is a short-cut to in-depth understanding and intimacy. She's simply not satisfied with friendship and orgasms. This woman's bedside manner will be Emily Post in style. Her primness will control her body-language, and this language will produce excitement similar to that of watching the grass grow.

If you feel impelled to cope with this idiotic language, your "pitch" should be short and curt; you will refuse to accept the nonsense as being appropriate. This female just needs reassurance to overcome her resistance. But you will expend enormous energy in this reassurance. This energy might be better spent meeting another woman.

One of the supreme delights of being single and a

rebach is to be the object of a female's aggressions. The aggressive, dedicatedly outspoken female is rare, but if you are lucky, you will find one.

"Let's not crap around with a lot of boring conversation. Let's go to bed."

She demands little except physical staying power, and she is a willing and frequent subject, provided your techniques are reasonably imaginative. The results are always entirely in your hands. If you want it, you can have it, if you are willing to burn the energy.

There are females who must be avoided like a raging hurricane. They are best described as under-educated females with overly expressed opinions on all things, and, unfortunately, violent opinions on most. You will quickly find yourself drenched in a storm of words. They opine constantly. It is best to walk a very wide circle around them because, unfortunately, they tend to continue these debates into situations (like bed) where debating ceases to be comfortable and, in any event, is the wrong kind of noise.

As a group, actresses, ballet dancers, and singers, operatic or otherwise, are super energetic. They use up almost all of their energy in professional situations, and by the time they become bedmates they really have little left, though they continue to perform because this is their training. Also, picture orgasm just complete and this artist reaching for the phone to call her agent.

There are females that are described as tough. Understanding a tough female requires your meeting one. All the descriptions you have heard will never define clearly "tough." These women are not particularly strong, nor are they dykes or professional wrestlers or boxers. They do have several characteristics in common. They're hungry and demanding and the world's greatest planners, seeking to consume all your time and energy. Do they ever demand, and there is never an end to it! And they know who to lean on—you!

In connection with them all, marshal your tactics, raise your defenses, and recognize the prey. The prey is you.

There are multiple other groupings—age, religion, previous conditions of servitude, ethnic background, color—but these all come together under one of the preceding fundamental characterizations.

There are subtle nuances in your behavior that can be used for various purposes.

For instance, carrying a large bankroll and spending as little as possible will be treated, generally, as an idiosyncrasy, and, as you know, idiosyncrasies are permissible among the rich.

Gamesmanship in speech can be used profitably.

"I am totally honest. When our relationship is ended, the bridge is burned, there's no way back." This puts you in a position of being able to walk away and at the same time leave with honor, saying if you must, "But remember baby, I warned you."

Of course, this can occur in reverse, and when it does, "*C'est la vie.*"

There is no substitute for the big lie and you will never be able to lie big enough. If properly done, there is nothing like a good, clean-cut lie that can still make you feel almost honest, if not honorable. For instance, most females think of themselves as special if endowed by you with a nickname. This technique can become complex depending on the number of nicknames used with numerous women. It's easy to forget who goes with what. It is well to choose one nickname every woman will like and use it all the time. If you call every woman "Tiger," you will never screw up, except when a woman calls you on the telephone and says:

"Hi there. This is Tiger!"

It is still better to take that risk than to fool around with a series of nicknames for each woman. (A course in voice recognition is very useful and is a solution.) Another clean-cut American lie that has withstood the test of time is "I love you."

All women like to receive presents. All women enjoy receiving them just prior to sex. Just afterwards makes no sense. Handle this by going to a friendly wholesale jeweler and purchasing small pins on a quantity basis, all exactly alike (just in case you are called upon to recollect what you have given somebody). Keep them handy, and whenever you deem it appropriate, pull one out and say very shyly and unoriginally:

"I bought this with you in mind."

All women enjoy a mistaken belief that there is something known as "woman's intuition," a private brand of ESP enjoyed only by them, to which no man can ever be party. It looks well if you can allow this idiotic intuition to work. There is nothing quite like a woman's intuitive feelings. Women will convince themselves of their great love feelings and know that, even though you said nothing, you surely feel the same. Don't bother dissuading them, use their intuition.

Be aware of the special quality in all women's language and conversation (i.e., stop signs that are bright go-ahead green). Classic statements in this category probably existed fifty years ago and still exist today:

"No. No. Stop!"

"I had too much to drink. I'm too tired.

"What will you think of me?"

"I'm not the type."

There are phrases that will serve you well, but they are such clichés that you may have difficulty uttering them. In the distant past you used them—by way of refreshing your recollection:

"If you love me, you'd show me by . . ."

"Are you a dyke or something?"

"You can't leave me like this."

And, the ultimate:

"You've got to do something to help me."

"I'm in terrible pain."

"We've gone too far. I can't stop."

If the woman believes you, it is because she wants to make love and needs an excuse and is able to think that physically she has saved you from the torments of temporary celibacy. Frankly, she just wants to feel like the local Red Cross nurse.

She will also feel that, in her own tantalizing (sarcasm intended) manner, she has created this impossible physical condition by her great sensuality; hence, the responsibility to relieve you will be hers.

It is hard to deal conceptually with screwing. Under ordinary circumstances, it should be as natural as shaking hands (we are told). However, what is natural to you is not necessarily natural to the screwee. (As a matter of fact, it is even possible to run an unacceptable debate on exactly who is, in fact, the screwer and who is, in fact, the screwee.) Nevertheless, for your purposes, you must always assume that you are doing the fucking, not that you are being fucked. Physically, that is.

If you have any doubts about how to screw, read a book. Any book will give you the basic differentiation between perversion and fun. There should be no rules. There also should be no pain. If you are inhibited by rules originating from upbringing, background, or lack of sexual education or experience, you probably can, with some effort, overcome all of them.

When seducing, don't necessarily attempt to accomplish the perfect scene. It is not necessary to be naked in bed with the lights low and the music soft. It is, initially, sufficient if you can get enough clothes off so that you can act. Once having overcome that barrier, making proper love is simple, and over a period of time all of the multitude of positions and movements will be available.

Sex, whether it is soft or passionate, must be played by ear. It is important that you understand that a man can always tune into a woman's excitement, but do not expect a woman to tune into a man's excitement.

All women enjoy a gentle, time-consuming approach. You are probably not accustomed to using this approach either because you were married too young or because, by the time your marriage ended, the boredom of it all was more than you could handle. It is an approach that should be used at length and regularly.

To many women, a threat of violence can be extraordinarily exciting. In circumstances like this, remember that violence is not supposed to hurt to the point of being actually painful. It is supposed to achieve a level of sexual ecstasy. Listen for the woman's words when you are making love. Hear her conversation. Hear her sounds. The tip-off will be there. Words like:

"I like a strong man."

"A man will always dominate a woman."

Or perhaps her body language will give the appearance of a struggle, but a struggle that is not too serious. (If she hauls off and slugs you, she's not kidding. Stop.)

Never appear to be in a hurry.

Never grab.

Never fumble. In other words, never appear that it has been too long since you have had a woman. Simply stated, don't ever act as if you've got your cock caught in a zipper and are waiting for a blueprint to get it out.

These miscellaneous generalities are applicable to all female alliances.

It is possible, under normal circumstances, to maintain about three deep, meaningful relationships at once. (Four, if two of the four are airline stewardesses; their profession keeps them out of town for reasonable periods of time.) At all times, let each of these various women know that she is not the only one, but that she is more important than the others.

Don't give out keys to your apartment, and, with respect to your apartment, while you are running these various relationships, don't let any woman leave her clothes around, particularly nightgowns on the back of bathroom doors. To many females, this is like staking a claim in the Klondike Gold Mine areas and, in *their* heads at least, posting a no trespassing sign to other females.

Charge accounts are useful for buying things spontaneously when you are with them, but disastrous if you loan the cards to them.

Presents purchased from time to time will keep your house in order and allow them to feel special.

Permitting them to do favors for you and your being "eternally grateful" will endear you to them.

Appearing helpless in picking ties and, more dramatically, clothes and allowing them to assist is a great relationship-improving tactic, provided they haven't got lousy taste. If their taste is bad, don't ask for help.

Allowing them to arrange, cook, and run your dinner parties and play hostess is worthwhile, especially if they think that the evening, rather than being just a social occasion, is crucial to your business advancement and that they are critical to the success of the venture.

Spreading these various joys among your various women should keep them all happy and you, as a result, amply buffered from the serious side of any relationship. Don't ever think or say "I don't play games" because where you are at is strictly gamesmanship. If they participate in the game, don't ever think that they don't understand that it is gamesmanship. If, in fact, she doesn't understand, and it becomes obvious she doesn't understand, fire her from the team and bring in a substitute. There are plenty of substitutes on the bench.

·16·

German Shepherds Are Companions Also

The curtain rises on the last act of your play as a reconditioned rebach male and finds you fully bored. The joy of sex, though no less joyous, is no longer the sole major driving force in your life. It ceases to dominate your thinking totally. It ceases to require your being a team player. What it requires is the one thing you have studiously avoided up to now because the idea was repellent. You are faced with the need for a relationship (or maybe just a companion).

The names in your personal telephone book are no longer interesting. You spend considerable time anticipating meetings with new females and being disillusioned after having met them, even though, out of habit or instinct, you will still pursue them to bed.

Your perpetual need to have female company as often as possible has dissipated. The new focus is a need for permanence, a need for sharing (more than just a bed), a need for loyalty, a need to dedicate yourself to one female. All of this does not mean that the first female who comes along right now is a woman you might marry. As a matter of fact, there's no reason to consider remarrying. Shacking up is an accepted and worthwhile enough lifestyle. But overall, you are ready for one woman, that is to say, one woman at a time.

And a temporary or tentative commitment is about to befall you.

This brings about various and sundry complications, for when you say to yourself, "Congratulations, you've got a roommate," you had better also be able to say to yourself, "Congratulations, you've got some nifty new problems."

For starters, children are going to be more of a problem when they are hers and not yours. Whether you move in or she moves in, if she brings a child with her, you become, depending on the age of the child, a strong male figure somewhere between a step- and/or surrogate father. The care and handling of your own children rarely prepares you for this new role.

You will spend an enormous amount of time in attempting to gain the friendship of the new child. You will discipline the child with great timidity and trepidation, resulting, probably, in lousy discipline. It will take you quite a while before you can handle the child as you would your own. In the interim, he/she has become extremely spoiled and difficult. But if you're clever and lucky through the hellish orientation period, the child may learn to like you—perhaps even more when you are just being your plain, old, ordinary ornery self than when you are trying self-consciously to impress a small friend.

The child will probably accept fairly quickly the fact

that you and his mother sleep in the same bed, primarily because the outside influences affecting the child are now limited (presumably the child's father will not be around to express an opinion on the housing accommodations).

Your children may be a different ballgame altogether.

They will, for the most part, be used to your total attention when they are around, and for a while you will be attentive to them, even with your new roommate present. Ultimately, your behavior will bring your female friend, her children, and your children into a semblance of a family situation.

Keep in mind that your children's mother will not be as tolerant of your relationship with this new woman as this woman's ex-husband might be. Despite the fact that your ex-wife may be living with another man, she will find occasion to comment negatively on your new relationship and the woman herself. As a general rule, in a situation like this women do not protect their species. They enjoy attacking each other.

Men don't and it's part of the same old locker room ethic.

A good deal of your success depends on your roommate's nature and on her attitude and approach toward your children. Hopefully, she will maintain subdued interest and enthusiasm, without too much lavish adoration and attention.

If you have never had children and have spent only an occasional hour or two with a niece or nephew, you are poorly prepared for what you are about to undertake with your new female's children.

If the child is an infant, you are fortunate, for all you have to do is occasionally pick it up (when the child is clean and neat), buy a copy of Dr. Spock, and make sure that there's a friendly pediatrician available. Also, you don't ever panic.

If the child is at the age gently described by department stores as toddlers, anticipate a difficult time. A toddler is a small person who can, with incredible ease, scale tables and couches, work on electrical plugs and outlets, and approach pills as though they were packaged by M&M. The woman will probably be able to accept many of these antics tranquilly because she can anticipate the extent of the child's ability, or at least she says she can. If a child starts to climb, your best approach (one highly thought of by the American Red Cross and various first aid courses) simply is to stop it! If a child is capable of finding pills, then consider yourself a damn idiot if you don't have them properly locked in an impregnable safe, and if a child gets near electric outlets, hit it (on the hand gently).

The age of fun starts around four and runs to twelve.

If you can stand the confusion and the general mess, you may have a ball. They can become amusing companions very quickly. Of course, don't overdo it, or your new little friends can also become dedicated pains in the neck.

From twelve on (until they move out), the problems

are so complex, enormous, and involved that it is best that you not be forewarned. Keep a psychiatrist's phone number handy. Not for them, but for you.

Involved, of course, in all this may be the parents. Hers and yours. Hopefully, all four of them have been prepared for this move. Prepared by you for yours and by her for hers. Presumably, you have met her parents casually and maybe, with luck, they have liked you (sort of), and presumably she has met your parents and they have liked her (sort of). Possibly, you have not become to her parents "what's his name" and she has not become to your parents "that woman."

Do not under any circumstances invite all four to dinner together, either at home or out. Unless, of course, your female is overly confident, or, and this is imperative, doesn't give a good goddamn. The pressure on any female living in circumstances like this is overwhelming. In any event, don't spend time babying or protecting her; at the very least she'd better be able to handle parents.

Problems with parents will have a good deal to do with the relative ages of the two people involved. It is likely that the female you are involved with may be younger, perhaps considerably younger than you, which means that your parents might conceivably be old enough to be her grandparents and her parents might be young enough to call you sir.

Attending family functions, weddings, communions, parties, funerals, and the like really is best avoided. It is nothing more than display time for either you or her, and who needs that. (Displaying her is O.K., just don't you get displayed.)

If there are children, moving around requires babysitters or nurses or a place to park the kids. Vacations will require the same planning or an extra ticket, an extra room, and certainly extra expense. But, be warned, your relationship will not survive unless high on the priority list are opportunities for the two of you to get away from the children.

Your lifestyle may also change dramatically in the furniture area—rearranging the room, disposing of and replacing old furniture and upholstery. For instance, the dining room table you didn't want because you preferred a bar will reappear, and the bar will go into storage.

Save the bar; it may be needed again.

And her furniture—a collection of pink frills, matching bedspreads and drapes, small chairs, and heavy marble tables—will overload the apartment at the cost of your outstanding decorating. You will either have to store her furniture and pay the bill or effect some integration of yours and hers and store some of each. It's best that you maintain the male tone of your apartment and the hell with integration.

However you handle the problem, do not sell off what appears to be excessive furniture, for in the event that your roommate and you part company, replacement costs will be extravagantly more than temporary storage costs.

Incidentally, all those cigarette lighters that you had that don't work will quickly be replaced by hers that do; a fantastic bonus if you smoke.

There are various possibilities to be considered when funding this operation. You can pay the freight yourself, a noble heroic gesture, particularly if you have the money. You can, in the interest of equal rights, divide all living bills on an equal basis. You can also pool your funds. As an example, you could pay the rent and buy the food to be eaten at home. If she has her own walking-around money, the money that you pool can be used for vacations, recreation and the like. (As a matter of fact, you don't even have to buy all the food that you eat in the house. That can be considered part of the pooling.)

Any one of these fiscal approaches assumes at all times that she is working or, if not working, has substantial money, an allowance or an inheritance of considerable funds.

The one thing that you do not do is set up a joint bank account. This is fraught with obvious dangers, both psychological and economical. It is better, even in this era of 7.9% interest compounded daily, to pool your money in a handy old-fashioned teapot and spend it as you go. If that seems impractical, then both of you should have separate bank accounts from which you draw and pay.

Overriding all other considerations is the basic fact that you have spent years handling money; hence, you should continue to do so. The average woman is insane with money and checking accounts and absolutely dense when income tax time arrives and she's made no provisions with regard to taxes. Women primarily are talented at spending what's on hand. That's their form of budgeting.

Obviously, in pooling, each buys his own clothes and jewelry.

Eventually, either with your first roommate or subsequent roommates, you will find one to whom you are more attached than the others and you will contemplate marriage. You will contemplate marriage for many reasons, the strongest of them being the need for permanency or a shared desire to have children. Even with all of the experience you have now logged as a single man (hopefully this has taken a period of a year at the minimum), you will still face a special set of problems before you can truly enjoy the status of ex-divorcé, or retired rebach.

Even though sufficient time has passed for you to ignore the warning that states that the woman in a second marriage is merely a rough carbon copy of the woman in the first, you will, of course, be gun-shy. And this state will inevitably bring you to the idea of an ante-nuptial agreement, for having once suffered the personal and financial agonies of divorce, an agreement, you think, will protect you from the economics of another such disaster. But ultimately you won't pursue the idea, because an ante-nuptial agreement does not allow you to fix alimony and possible child support in advance. The law doesn't allow it because an agreement like this is considered to be against the public interest. It is against the public interest because it is an agreement that contemplates divorce and contemplating divorce in advance of marriage is considered immoral. All an antenuptial agreement promises is that your future wife will not seek any part of your estate after you are dead because she will have enough money to support herself then without taking what you leave behind. Frankly, since the agreement only takes effect after you are dead, it can hardly affect your life, so why bother. It is a useful document only if you have an awful lot of kids from a previous marriage and very limited means of providing for them after you are dead. It can, however, have an effect on your future wife to the extent that it challenges in advance what appears to be, so far, a perfectly harmonious relationship.

Rare is the woman who will contemplate fondly the idea that she may be a "gold digger," though it is a term you should be aware of. The term exists because such women exist. Draw up a document anyhow, however, if she'll sign it. List in it what you'll give her in the event of a divorce even if it angers her. She'll want the marriage so bad she'll sign. Even if it's not valid, chances are she'll abide by it, and, in any event, the law may change.

·17·

When All the Words to All the Songs Seem True

This woman with whom you have chosen to share your bed and board—if she is to become a permanent fixture in your life—should possess two overriding characteristics.

First, she should be, for as long as your relationship lasts, your best friend, in the fullest sense of the word. Also, your confidante, sounding board, and advisor, as well as the one person from whom you can count on dedicated honesty (even when she knows such honesty may be painful to you; upon hearing it, you will often know that she is wrong but you cannot convince her she's wrong).

It is a relationship that should replace all other best friends you may have at the time, including that large pack of currently single men with whom you have been traveling. This doesn't mean that you will be giving up your friends, but rather that your involvement with them will be considerably reduced. If you have any doubts about the need for this reduction, then this is the time to entertain doubts about the permanency of your relationship with this woman. If she has things in proper perspective, she will certainly not seek to keep you from enjoying relationships with your friends, relationships that more than likely will require your having, on a frequent basis, the "boys' night out."

These are nights to be enjoyed without guilt, unlike those during your first marriage, provided they are scheduled so that if she chooses to go out, she can do so on a planned basis. They should not be nights suddenly created at the last minute because one of the "old gang" calls you and makes a crack that forces you to prove something. Hopefully, your ego at this point is secure enough to accept lines such as:

"Do you mean that you need her permission?"

"Hell, is she afraid you might meet a woman?"

"It seems to me that's why you got divorced in the first place!"

"Guilty already?"

"You just can't walk out on your old friends."

Once you have settled in with a woman and begun a long hibernation, other inappropriate remarks, politely called chiding, but not funny, will surface:

"Wasn't once enough?"

"You finally broke down and she finally got you."

"She's pregnant!"

By this time, you should have reached the point of no longer asking "Am I really in love?" but rather have established in your own head the answer to that oft-asked question. Your answer is that you enjoy being with her; there are good vibes, and it does really boil down to the fact that she is your best friend.

This profile is complete if you can add to the merits of

friendship the fact that she fucks like a mink. The greatest single antitoxin to the bad marriage virus is great sex, and it is not a chicken-and-egg question. It is awfully difficult for open, comfortable, energetic, enjoyable sex to be loused up by the nitty-gritty of day-to-day living. Sex can at all times be a defense against boredom, the terminal disease of marriage. Sex can at all times be, especially in a double bed, a defense against extended bickering that can turn into destructive misunderstanding. If you bicker your way into bed, good sex should be able to end the heated words.

Unlike your first wife, the new potential spouse may face a problem of identity. Do not educate her beyond the level she has already achieved. An educated best friend winds up as your personal college professor, lecturing on a condescending level.

When you first got married, Gloria Steinem, Germaine Greer, Kate Millett, Betty Friedan, and Company, were writing, but their declarations of female independence were yet unpublished. They have propounded, among other things, education for women, and this is fine—educate all women everywhere, but do not educate wives. Perhaps by the time you were divorced or divorcing, they had just exploded on the scene and were still considered by many males, including you, a fringe lunatic group. Their postures and attitudes had at most a barely discernible influence on the attitudes and actions of your first wife. (They are, of course, now no longer a fringe group.)

The identity of a woman to the woman herself can be

a major marital problem, particularly if it reaches the
level of crisis, which means that she hasn't figured out
where she's at; marriage to you isn't going to clarify
anything, much less do anything positive for you. Her
crisis is considerably relieved if you can give value to
her role as a housewife, unexpressed openly, but still
maintain the theory of "barefoot and pregnant." It may
not be fair, but, if well expressed, it can keep her loy-
al and happy, and if she's not happy, at least you'll
be.

As mentioned earlier, it is possible your new woman
will be substantially younger than you, and this age
difference can be the basis for a crisis. In the beginning
of this relationship, you may find yourself in the position of teacher, introducing her to new places and new
things. In short, a brand new way of life; particularly
true if she has never been married before. And, in the
beginning, she may accept and enjoy her new life.

But as sure as day follows night, she will at some
point begin to seek value and meaning in her new life,
which can never be filled by mere mortal man, particularly you. To forestall this problem, you must start
early. She must be encouraged to develop real, not
artificial, interests, interests that you do not consider
unworthy. But she must be treated in the same fashion
you would treat a talented child. Break your ass to
encourage her to develop that talent, but keep yourself
as the paramount force in her life. As with children, give
her her rights, lots of rope, but pull her up short when
she loses sight of her primary goal—you!

If she has not completed school and she wants to,

move in that direction, not simply for the initials she can apply to the end of her name, but rather to enhance her money-making ability. Encourage it. Do not encourage school without this purpose (i.e., anthropology, philosophy, etc.), for an identity crisis can best be resolved by meaningful, rewarding, gainful employment. The money she earns you don't have to, and you both can spend.

If she appears uninterested in doing anything but taking care of you, she has either resolved the question of identity or never faced it. In the former case (if true), terrific. In the latter case, you have a problem because the question will eventually develop. You must make her feel that her identity and yours are merged and that she does not need one of her own.

As much as you might like to think that starting a family may be the answer to her restlessness or, if you already have one, that it should be sufficient), such judgment should be closely examined.

But if you have stumbled upon a woman whose total interest in life will be to take care of you, beware of the truth. You don't need anything near the care that this woman thinks you need. Hopefully, she will realize that her identity is more than a social security number.

Consider children. If you have a set and she has a set, you really don't need a joint set. Your marriage will survive beautifully just on the quantities that are around. If, however, you have developed a relationship with a childless female (who is childless so far by choice), then, if she is young enough, hope that even if she should protest that she does not want children, she will be a happy stepmother to those that you have. Also, accept the fact that this is not the way it is going to be for long. At some point, she is going to want to go through the miseries of pregnancy, taking you along into areas you probably never experienced in your earlier marriage. The worst of these is natural childbirth with you "helping." In spite of all the beautiful things ever written about helping a woman deliver a child, unless you are attuned to blood, pain, and modern medicine, don't contemplate it any more than you would contemplate jumping off a high bridge. It is *not* beautiful, and you will *not* be helpful. It is far wiser, if you find yourself faced with the Lamaze Method, to do it the old-fashioned way. Pace around a waiting room until the doctor comes in and tells you what you've got, appear briefly at your wife's side after she has been cleaned up, smile benignly, and cry or cheer. Just don't be involved as a helper. Considering what you pay the doctor, he certainly doesn't need your help.

It is true that this may sound hard-nosed. It is true that she is in pain. It is true that all you are doing is comforting her. It is also true, and both you and your wife should understand, that you will come out of all this as a basket case. The testimony from parents who have gone through it, namely, that the husbands love it, is total propaganda.

If you have never had children, their production is worth undertaking. All things being equal, and in spite of their destructive abilities, the troops are O.K. (most of the time).

It is inconceivable that religion as a problem has not, by this time, been compromised or handled intellectually. If, however, there are religious differences and these differences have never been confronted, the time for that confrontation is now. Without attempting to cover all the religious match-ups that can create problems, it is obvious that problems will exist in any dissimilar religious joining. Those same problems may very well exist in a relationship between two persons of the same religion when the nature of the religion is not clearly understood. Jewish orthodoxy can hardly be compared to Jewish reform. This is equally true of Catholic orthodoxy and just plain old-fashioned once-in-a-while confession Catholicism.

Approach it. Face it. Resolve it. Failure to resolve or to clear a path is an invitation to marital suicide. If she thinks she loves you enough, she'll probably convert to your religion, if you think it's important enough. If it has no special meaning to you, let the chips fall where they may.

As for money, it would appear that the only thing you need do with it is to agree between yourselves how to spend it. As a divorcé, you, of course, are committed to alimony and support payments. These should prove not too formidable when your sole concern is to have a good time. But, when taking on another woman, you must face the spending problem realistically. You and your new friend must clearly understand exactly what you, in fact, do earn. But more than just the fancy size of your earnings, there must be total and absolute clarity about the outflow and what is left after ex-wives, children, and income taxes. Handled early, this subject can prove painless. Handled late, it can prove destructive. If the female you find is working, part of the solution to the financial situation should be that she continues to work.

The entire subject of money must from the start be treated by you in the role of dictator. You should consult with her, but you must reserve the ultimate rights of decision. While you earn, you must control it. Failing that, you may never earn enough.

If you have found an heiress, you will enjoy her funds with her, avoid making any big deal about the fact that she has more money than you are ever going to earn, and laugh on the way to the bank at any ex-friends who make obvious remarks.

The basic woman you are seeking has been labeled "total." Those women who believe in the "Total Woman" should work out fine as partners. There is nothing wrong with daily pampering. There is nothing wrong with a martini waiting for you properly mixed and iced when you arrive home. There is everything right about a woman spending time addressing herself to the matters of provocative clothing, esoteric foods, and extraordinary sexual acrobatics.

Unfortunately, there is also the E.R.A. You will find this constitutional amendment difficult to handle and probably not worth the effort. If you are faced with it in its extreme, do not attempt to be liberal, liberated, or even reasonable. You have probably chosen badly. If this attitude has been concealed, you've erred in not forcing it to the surface. It is not that equal rights for women is unconscionable; as a matter of fact, in many respects it places you in a powerful position when it comes to potential future support and alimony. It is simply that a militant defender of the E.R.A. will also be a ball-busting militant woman and/or wife.

·18·

To Be or Not to Be
Is No Longer in Question

And so you have achieved the status of full-fledged, totally liberated and comfortable rebach.

What has it all meant?

It should have been a learning experience. Some of the lessons learned have been harsh and some bitter, but all should be remembered.

In the first place, you should know by this time that love is a story that ends in the first chapter because in the second chapter love becomes a weary, plodding, tiresome concept.

You should have learned, at the very least, that just as a camel is a horse worked out by compromise, so also a marriage is nothing more than a relationship worked out by compromise. It is an answer to nothing. It can barely be justified on the basis that there are no other alternatives and, even then, the justification for marriage appears to tie directly into bearing and raising children.

By this time, certain things should have become axiomatic. People who are committed to each other don't have to be handcuffed or Siamese twins. You should realize that you need space and that infidelity is probably one of the prerequisites for this space.

Further axioms include the positive idea that when a woman loses a husband or boyfriend she loses more than a man loses in the same analogous situation.

For many men, divorce, unfortunately, is the first life-experience that kicks them in the ass. Handling a kick in the ass on any occasion is difficult, and this is no better. For other males, who have consistently been shoved around and fought back, divorce can be somewhat less ponderous, but no less painful.

From the day of the slammed door to where you are now, you should have had occasion to sort out the loose ends of your former life. You should have discovered where things went awry; whether in fact it was the female (it no doubt was), or the sex, or your attitude, or any one of the innumerable things that make life what it is.

But at least now you have given yourself another chance. You have conceivably decided to remarry, or you have decided that you are going to stay single. In either case, you should have decided what you want, and where you want your life to go, married or otherwise. In that connection, your goals should be short term, for any decision made today can be changed tomorrow. You must never forget that even though you think you have learned all that there is to learn about women and marriage and un-marriage, there is no reason for remarriage, even if you think you have all the understanding necessary.

Merle Shain has written:

.TO BE OR NOT TO BE.

It's seasonal work being single and you never know how long your season will be, nor can you direct whether Spring will follow Winter, you just have to wait and hope and see.

Wait and hope and see.

Waiting dissipates impatience. Discarded impatience protects against a hurried effort to fill your well of loneliness with just any female, and maybe the need to bring in that one and only female will never arise. Maybe, just maybe, there can be quality in quantity and the season for being single is the only season of the year.

You are now standing on a mountain and calling it a mole hill. Probably the view and your trip there were as much accident as hard work.

Norman Savage has written:

> And when it's time
> The breezes will come,
> as they always have,
> without any help from you. If
> they be soft and warm consider
> yourself lucky that somebody,
> something had the sense
> to make a liar out of all of us.

No longer do you have to hide under the bed and claim you were playing hide and seek. No longer do you have to think in terms of ''affairs,'' ''relationships,'' or that boring gray area in which you were referred to as a divorcé. These are society's phrases that are supposed to simplify everything and are really just cheap shots. These ideas belong to an archaic lifestyle and are a part of your ancient history. None of these thoughts are part of the renaissance man, and you have become the renaissance man.

By this time, there should be very few leftover remnants of anger toward the Bitch of Buchenwald. In its place should repose a comfortable indifference. Remorse and guilt over the children should have gone the way of the great zeppelins. Guilt with regard to your former marriage should at this point have also joined the zeppelin fleet.

There is little about divorce that can be treated as something good because you have been cheated out of many years, out of much happiness, and considerable money and possessions. But there are things that will come out of it that are rewarding. You abandoned a disastrous marriage and a putrid lifestyle. At the very least, you learned something about yourself and developed a new image.

And you have learned about anger, insightful anger, raging anger, an anger you can handle without liquor or drugs to deaden its pain. An anger that you now understand and has become controllable and comfortable.

Loneliness, though around occasionally, exists now without intensity because you've filled your life; and with the fall of loneliness so too has anxiety collapsed.

And surely by this time, all of the crazy, wild, mixed-up emotions, characterized as often as not by such things as older children hating you and vowing they are never going to see you again or the bleak despair of your first crummy apartment, are behind you, forgotten and lost.

There is no time for comparison. There is only time to look forward and enjoy what you are doing, much of which enjoyment has been on the back of the mistakes you made the first time around.

All the time spent in rebacheloring should subtotal:

Look out for number one—and that number belongs to you.

Getting "the lion's share" requires consummate greed and creative gluttony. There can never be (nor should there ever be) enough.

The apex of the lion's share should be the desire and the ability to remain single, which is a permanent opportunity to be devotedly selfish and self-indulgent. This can be a life of total grandeur.

Singleness can only be fully savored when it occurs after marriage because it is total freedom without compromise. It follows a married life of constant concession (yours). Any female intrusion of a permanent nature is a disruption of this freedom.

Epilogue

DECLARATION OF INDEPENDENCE, 1776
(In Part)

When in the course of human events, it becomes necessary for one *people to dissolve* the political *bands which have connected them with another, and to assume* among the powers of the earth, *the separate and equal station* to *which the laws of nature and of nature's God entitle them, a decent respect to the opinions of mankind requires that they should declare the causes which impel them to the separation.*

We hold these truths to be self-evident, *that all men are created equal, that they are endowed by their Creator with certain unalienable rights, that among these are life, liberty and the pursuit of happiness—* That to secure these rights, governments are instituted among men, deriving their just powers from the consent of the governed, that whenever any form of government becomes destructive of these ends, it is the right of the people to alter or to abolish it, and to institute a new government, laying its foundation on such principles and organizing its powers in such form, as to them shall seem most likely to effect their safety and happiness. Prudence, indeed, will dictate that governments long established should not be changed for light and transient causes; and accordingly *all experience hath shewn, that mankind are more disposed to suffer, while evils are sufferable, than to right themselves by abolishing the forms to which they are accustomed. But when a long train of abuses and usurpations, pursuing invariably the same object, evinces a design to reduce them under absolute despotism, it is their right, it is their duty, to throw off such government, and to provide new guards for their future security.*